40-Day Journey with Maya Angelou

Other books in the

40-DAY *Journey*
Series

40-Day Journey with Joan Chittister
Beverly Lanzetta, Editor

40-Day Journey with Dietrich Bonhoeffer
Ron Klug, Editor

40-Day Journey with Martin Luther
Gracia M. Grindal, Editor

40-Day Journey with Kathleen Norris
Kathryn Haueisen, Editor

40-Day Journey with Parker J. Palmer
Henry F. French, Editor

40-Day Journey with Julian of Norwich
Lisa E. Dahill, Editor

40-Day Journey with Madeleine L'Engle
Isabel Anders, Editor

40-Day Journey with Gerard Manley Hopkins
Francis X. McAloon, S.J., Editor

40-Day Journey with Howard Thurman
Donna F. Schaper, Editor

40-DAY

Journey

WITH MAYA ANGELOU

40-Day Journey Series

Henry F. French, Editor

Augsburg Books

Minneapolis

Cover art: Photo © Dwight Carter Photography
Cover design: Laurie Ingram
Interior design: PerfecType, Nashville, Tenn.

Library of Congress Cataloging-in-Publication Data

40-day journey with Maya Angelou / Henry F. French, editor.
    p. cm. -- (40-day journey series)
  Includes bibliographical references and index.
  ISBN 978-0-8066-5770-7 (alk. paper)
  1. Devotional exercises. 2. Angelou, Maya. I. French, Henry F.
  BV4832.3.A16 2009
  204'.3208996073--dc22

2009032362

The paper used in this publication meets the minimum requirements of American National Standard for Information Sciences—Permanence of Paper for Printed Library Materials, ANSI Z329.48-1984.

Printed in Canada

CONTENTS

Series Introduction

Imagine spending forty days with a great spiritual guide who has both the wisdom and the experience to help you along the path of your own spiritual journey. Imagine being able to listen to and question spiritual guides from the past and the present. Imagine being, as it were, mentored by women and men who have made their own spiritual journey and have recorded the landmarks, detours, bumps in the road, potholes, and wayside rests that they encountered along the way—all to help others (like you) who must make their own journey.

The various volumes in Augsburg Books' *40-Day Journey Series* are all designed to do just that—to lead you where your mind and heart and spirit long to go. As Augustine once wrote: *"You have made us for yourself, O Lord, and our heart is restless until it rests in you."* The wisdom you will find in the pages of this series of books will give you the spiritual tools and direction to find that rest. But there is nothing quietistic in the spirituality you will find here. Those who would guide you on this journey have learned that the heart that rests in God is one that lives with deeper awareness, deeper creativity, deeper energy, and deeper passion and commitment to the things that matter to God.

An ancient Chinese proverb states the obvious: the journey of a thousand miles begins with the first step. In a deep sense, books in the *40-Day Journey Series* are first steps on a journey that will not end when the forty days are over. No one can take the first step (or any step) for you.

Imagine that you are on the banks of the Colorado River. You are here to go white-water rafting for the first time and your guide has just described the experience, telling you with graphic detail what to expect. It sounds both exciting and frightening. You long for the experience but are somewhat disturbed, anxious, uncertain in the face of the danger that promises to accompany you on the journey down the river. The guide gets into the raft. She will accompany you on the journey, *but she can't take the journey for you.* If you want to experience the wildness of the river, the raw beauty of the canyon, the camaraderie of adventurers, and the mystery of a certain oneness with nature (and nature's creator), then you've got to get in the boat.

This book in your hand is like that. It describes the journey, provides a "raft," and invites you to get in. Along with readings from your spiritual guide, you will find scripture to meditate on, questions to ponder, suggestions for personal journaling, guidance in prayer, and a prayer for the day. If done faithfully each day, you will find the wisdom and encouragement you need to integrate meaningful spiritual insights and practices into your daily life. And when the 40-day journey is over it no longer will be the guide's description of the journey that stirs your longing for God but *your own experience* of the journey that grounds your faith and life and keeps you on the path.

I would encourage you to pick up other books in the series. There is only one destination, but many ways to get there. Not everything in every book will work for you (we are all unique), but in every book you will find much to help you discover your own path on the journey to the One in whom we all "live and move and have our being" (Acts 17:28).

May all be well with you on the journey.
Henry F. French, Series Editor

PREFACE

To the delight of many and the consternation if not anger of many others, the United States has its first African-American First Family. Both the President and the First Lady have compelling life stories, stories with deep roots in Africa, stories inextricably linked to the tragedy and obscenity of American slavery, stories woven along with millions of other stories from threads of many colors into a tapestry called "Growing Up Black in America."

Both of their stories tell of strong women—mothers and grandmothers— whose deep love, values, faith, and hard work, not to mention idiosyncrasies, provided the cornerstones upon which they built their lives. Americans of whatever race—but perhaps particularly white Americans, if they are open to it—will learn much about what it means to be human and what it means to be American from hearing their stories. The same can be said of Maya Angelou.

Maya Angelou (born Marguerite Johnson) tells the story of her remarkable life in six autobiographies. They chronicle the story of her journey from toddlerhood in Arkansas under the tutelage of her maternal grandmother, through an often tumultuous quest for teenage identity in California with her feisty and unpredictable mother, to maturity as an African-American woman. Her story and the wisdom she picked up along the way—often painfully, frequently hilariously, always poignantly—does indeed speak to what it means to be human and what it means to be American.

Her journey has not been easy. America has not been an easy place to live and grow and prosper if you are black and poor and "exist sparingly on the mean side of the hill."[1] In her autobiographies, many volumes of poetry, books of essays, civil rights activism, and career as a singer and performer and director, Maya Angelou maps the physical, psychological, emotional, and spiritual territory that black Americans have lived in, and in many cases still live in. As Sharon Burt wrote, "The life and work of Maya Angelou are fully intertwined. Angelou's poetry and personal narratives form a larger picture wherein the symbolic Maya Angelou rises to become a point of consciousness for African-American people, especially black women seeking to survive masculine prejudice, in addition to whites' hatred of blacks and blacks lack of power."[2]

In many ways, the works of Maya Angelou are an undeniably important but not easy read. She unabashedly, and with an unapologetic eye for truth, pushes many hot buttons and evokes in her readers often visceral reactions of anger, guilt, shame, and despair, but also of hope and promise and a yearning for a more realized humanity, a deeper community and a less hateful and hurtful world.

Why would you want to spend forty days with Maya Angelou? Simply because she is Maya Angelou—an incomparably interesting person. A 40-day conversation with Maya Angelou about a variety of topics is bound to be both provocative and enriching. The questions to ponder and the suggestions for journaling will open up the conversation—a conversation that will take different readers to different places due to the particularities of each reader's life experience. Some of the daily readings and questions may prove particularly challenging—especially to white readers—but for those who stay in the conversation, there are gems to be mined from the life and work of Maya Angelou.

In the poem that opens this 40-day journey, Maya Angelou muses:

Why do we journey, muttering
like rumors among the stars?
Is a dimension lost?
Is it love?[3]

Her work and her life answer the question. In too much of our world love is indeed lost and the world is the worse for it; but here and there, in individual relationships, in families, in pockets of community, love is found and the world is the better for it. Should that love ever flow freely and genuinely between the races, the sexes, the classes, the ages perhaps we can stop our muttering journey and journey on in joy.

It is hoped that this little book will help school the reader in some of the beliefs, attitudes, behaviors and practices to be drawn from Maya Angelou's life and work that contribute to the healing of the world. As Maya Angelou's good friend African-American author and playwright James Baldwin wrote, in her work: "You will hear the regal woman, the mischievous street girl; you will hear the price of a black woman's survival and you will hear of her generosity. Black, bitter, and beautiful, she speaks of our survival."[4]

40-Day Journey with Maya Angelou is in every sense of the word a "sampler" of Maya Angelou's poetry, autobiographies, and essays. It is designed to whet your appetite and encourage you—when the forty days are over—to dive more deeply into her writing. And should you do just that, I suspect you will find yourself agreeing with Maya Angelou's self-assessment:

I am woman
Phenomenally.
Phenomenal woman
That's me.[5]

How to Use This Book

Your 40-day journey with Maya Angelou gives you the opportunity to be mentored by a great contemporary African-American poet, essayist, autobiographer, performer, teacher, and guide to the deep recesses of the human spirit. The purpose of the journey, however, is not just to gain "head knowledge" about Maya Angelou. Rather, it is to begin living what you learn from this remarkable woman.

You will probably benefit most by fixing a special time of day in which to "meet with" Maya Angelou. It is easier to maintain a spiritual practice if you do it regularly at the same time. For many people mornings, while the house is still quiet and before the busyness of the day begins, is a good time. Others will find that the noon hour or before bedtime serves well. We are all unique. Some of us are "morning people" and some of us are not. Do whatever works *for you* to maintain a regular meeting with Maya Angelou. Write it into your calendar and do your best to keep your appointments.

It is best if you complete your 40-day journey in forty days. A deepening focus and intensity of experience will be the result. However, it is certainly better to complete the journey than to give it up because you can't get it done in forty days. Indeed, making it a 40- or 20-week journey may better fit your schedule and it just might be that spending a whole week, or perhaps half a week, reflecting on the reading, the scripture, and the prayers, and then practicing what you are learning could be a powerfully transforming experience as well. Again, set a schedule that works for you, only be consistent.

Each day of the journey begins with a reading from Maya Angelou. You will note that the readings, from day to day, build on each other and introduce you to key ideas in her understanding of life, human relationships and faith. Read each selection slowly, letting the words sink into your consciousness. You may want to read each selection two or three times before moving on, perhaps reading it out loud once.

Following the reading from Maya Angelou's writings, you will find the heading *Biblical Wisdom* and a brief passage from the Bible that relates to what she has said. As with the selection from Angelou, read the biblical text slowly, letting the words sink into your consciousness.

Following the biblical reading, you will find the heading *Silence for Meditation.* Here you should take anywhere from five to twenty minutes meditating on the two readings. Begin by getting centered. Sit with your back straight, eyes closed, hands folded in your lap, and breathe slowly and deeply. Remember that breath is a gift of God, it is God's gift of life. Do nothing for two or three minutes other than simply observe your breath. Focus your awareness on the end of your nose. Feel the breath enter through your nostrils and leave through your nostrils.

Once you feel your mind and spirit settling down, open your eyes and read both the daily reading and the biblical text again. Read them slowly, focus on each word or phrase, savor them, explore possible meanings and implications. At the end of each day you will find a blank page with the heading *Notes.* As you meditate on the readings, jot down any insights that occur to you. Do the readings raise any questions for you? Write them down. Do the readings suggest anything you should do? Write it down.

Stay at it as long as it feels useful. When your mind is ready to move on, close your eyes and observe your breath for a minute or so. Then return to the book and the next heading: *Questions to Ponder.* Here you will find a few pointed questions by Henry French, the book's compiler and editor, on the day's reading. These are general questions intended for all spiritual seekers and communities of faith. Think them through and write your answers (and the implications of your answers for your own life of faith and for your community of faith) in the *Notes* section.

Many of these *Questions to Ponder* are designed to remind us—as Maya Angelou would affirm—that although spirituality is always personal, it is simultaneously relational and communal. A number of the questions, therefore, apply the relevance of the day's reading to faith communities. Just remember, a faith community may be as large as a regular organized gathering of any religious tradition, or as small as a family, or the relationship between spiritual friends. You don't need to be a member of a church, synagogue, mosque, or temple to be part of a faith community. Answer the questions in the context of your particular faith community.

Then move on to the heading *Psalm Fragment.* Here you will find a brief verse or two from the Hebrew book of Psalms that relate to the day's reading. The Psalms have always been the mainstay of prayer in the Christian tradition and always speak to the real situations in which we find ourselves—the kind of realism that Maya Angelou's teaching and life resonate with.

Reflect for a moment on the *Psalm Fragment* and then continue on to the heading *Journal Reflections*. Several suggestions for journaling are given that apply the readings to your own personal experience. It is in journaling that the "day" reaches its climax and the potential for transformative change is greatest. It would be best to buy a separate journal rather than use the *Notes* section of the book. For a journal you can use a spiral-bound or ring-bound notebook or one of the hardcover journal books sold in stationery stores. Below are some suggestions for how to keep a journal. For now, let's go back to the 40-day journey book.

The *Questions to Ponder* and *Journal Reflection* exercises are meant to assist you in reflecting on the daily reading and scripture quotations. Do not feel that you have to answer every question. You may choose which questions or exercises are most helpful to you. Sometimes a perfectly appropriate response to a question is, "I don't know" or "I'm not sure what I think about that." The important thing is to record your own thoughts and questions.

After *Journal Reflections*, you will find two more headings. The first is *Prayers of Hope & Healing*. One of the highest services a person of faith can perform is prayer for family and friends, for one's community of faith, for the victims of injustice, and for one's enemies. Under this heading you will find suggestions for prayer that relate to the key points in the day's readings. The last heading (before *Notes*) is *Prayer for Today*, a one or two line prayer to end your "appointment" with Maya Angelou, and to be prayed from time to time throughout the day.

Hints on Keeping a Journal

A journal is a very helpful tool. Keeping a journal is a form of meditation, a profound way of getting to know yourself—and God—more deeply. Although you could read your 40-day journey book and reflect on it "in your head," writing can help you focus your thoughts, clarify your thinking, and keep a record of your insights, questions, and prayers. Writing is generative: it enables you to have thoughts you would not otherwise have had.

A Few Hints for Journaling

1. Write in your journal with grace. Don't get stuck in trying to do it perfectly. Just write freely. Don't worry about literary style, spelling, or grammar. Your goal is simply to generate thoughts pertinent to your own life and get them down on paper.
2. You may want to begin and end your journaling with prayer. Ask for the guidance and wisdom of the Spirit (and thank God for that guidance and wisdom when you are done).
3. If your journaling takes you in directions that go beyond the journaling questions in your 40-day book, go there. Let the questions encourage, not limit, your writing.
4. Respond honestly. Don't write what you think you're supposed to believe. Write down what you really do believe, in so far as you can identify that. If you don't know, or are not sure, or if you have questions, record those. Questions are often openings to spiritual growth.
5. Carry your 40-day book and journal around with you every day during your journey (only keep them safe from prying eyes). The 40-day journey process is an intense experience that doesn't stop when you close the book. Your mind and heart and spirit will be engaged all day, and it will be helpful to have your book and journal handy to take notes or make new entries as they occur to you.

JOURNEYING WITH OTHERS

You can use your 40-day book with another person, a spiritual friend or partner, or with a small group. It would be best for each person to first do his or her own reading, reflection, and writing in solitude. Then when you come together, share the insights you have gained from your time alone. Your discussion will probably focus on the *Questions to Ponder;* however, if the relationship is intimate, you may feel comfortable sharing some of what you have written in your journal. No one, however, should ever be pressured to share anything in their journal if they are not comfortable doing so.

Remember that your goal is to learn from one another, not to argue or to prove that you are right and the other person wrong. Just practice listening and trying to understand why your partner, friend, or colleague thinks as he or she does.

Practicing intercessory prayer together, you will find, will strengthen the spiritual bonds of those who take the journey together. And as you all work to translate insight into action, sharing your experience with each other is a way of encouraging and guiding each other and provides the opportunity to provide feedback to each other gently if that becomes necessary.

CONTINUING THE JOURNEY

When the forty days (or forty weeks) are over, a milestone has been reached, but the journey needn't end. One goal of the 40-day series is to introduce you to a particular spiritual guide with the hope that, having whet your appetite, you will want to keep the journey going. At the end of the book are some suggestions for further reading that will take you deeper on your journey with your mentor.

Who Is Maya Angelou?

The woman that the world knows as Maya Angelou was born Marguerite Johnson on April 4, 1928. It was her brother Bailey who gave her the name Maya. When they were toddlers, he called her "My Sister." That was eventually shortened to "My" and then finally expanded to "Maya." In 1950, when she was twenty-two, Marguerite married a Greek sailor named Tosh Angelos. Although the marriage lasted only a few years, some years later when she was auditioning for a job as a calypso singer at the Purple Onion (a San Francisco nightclub), she needed a stage name. The final "s" on Angelos was dropped and replaced with a "u," and Marguerite Johnson became and has remained Maya Angelou.

Maya Angelou was three years old when her parents divorced and she, along with her brother, was sent by train from California to Stamps, Arkansas, to live with her grandmother, Annie Henderson. In Stamps, she encountered up close and personally the segregation and legally enforceable discrimination that characterized the South. It might easily have become a soul-crushing experience had her grandmother not instilled in her a certain pride and confidence in herself. Thanks to her feisty grandmother's strength of character, deep love, wisdom, and strong religious faith, the young Maya observed and internalized the values that accompanied her on the road to maturity.

After five years with their grandmother in Arkansas, Maya and Bailey went to live with their mother and extended family in St. Louis. Life with her mother, Vivian Baxter, was never dull, often chaotic, if not tempestuous, and quite unpredictable. As Maya wrote in her first autobiography, "To describe my mother would be to write about a hurricane in its perfect power. Of the climbing, falling colors of a rainbow."[6] The eight-year-old Maya found a modicum of refuge from the hurricane in books and comic books. She got her first library card in St. Louis, where she indulged her appetite for reading and laid the groundwork for the literary gems she would later produce.

While in St. Louis, Maya was first molested and then raped by her mother's boyfriend, a Mr. Freeman. When he had finished with her, the rapist warned her that if she told anyone what had happened he would kill her brother Bailey. When her mother and brother discovered that she had been raped, she at first refused out of fear for her brother's safety to say who had done it. Bailey, however, eventually got her to tell him. Mr. Freeman was arrested, tried, convicted, and sentenced to one year and one day in jail. He never served his time. His lawyer got him released the same day he was sentenced, and the next day he turned up dead—kicked to death, presumably by Maya's uncle (although that was never proven).

Maya, emotionally devastated by the whole experience, refused to talk to anyone but Bailey, believing that her words had caused Mr. Freeman's death. Eventually her refusal to talk became more than her mother and her St. Louis relatives could take, and she and Bailey were returned to Stamps and grandmother Henderson.

Back in Stamps, Maya continued in her self-imposed silence. As she wrote in her autobiography: "For nearly a year, I sopped around the house, the Store, the school and the church like an old biscuit, dirty and inedible."[7] Then she was taken into the mentoring care of Mrs. Bertha Flowers, "the aristocrat of Black Stamps,"[8] who told her one afternoon:

> Now no one is going to make you talk—possibly no one can. But bear in mind, language is man's way of communicating with his fellow man and it is language alone which separates him from the lower animals. . . . Your grandmother says you read a lot. Every chance you get. That's good, but not good enough. Words mean more than what is set down on paper. It takes the human voice to infuse them with the shades of deeper meaning.[9]

With great patience and considerable understanding of the ways of a young girl, Mrs. Flowers helped Maya regain the confidence and self-esteem that had been taken from her in St. Louis. She taught her to appreciate both the power of literature and the power of the spoken word, and brought both lessons together in her conviction that especially poetry needs to be spoken, not just written on a page and read—a lesson reflected in Maya Angelou the poet's adult work.

In 1940, Maya and Bailey moved from Stamps to San Francisco to live with their mother. It was a turbulent period and it soon proved too much for her. She went to live with her father and his girlfriend in a ramshackle trailer park. She soon discovered that life with her father was no improvement over life with her mother, and she ran away to spend a month living with other homeless children of many racial backgrounds, scavenging in a junkyard and sleeping in abandoned automobiles. It was a hardscrabble life but one which taught the adolescent Maya some important lessons:

> After a month my thinking processes had so changed that I was hardly recognizable to myself. The unquestioning acceptance by my peers had dislodged the familiar insecurity. Odd that the homeless children, the silt of war frenzy, could initiate me into the brotherhood of man. After hunting down unbroken bottles and selling them with a white girl from Missouri, a Mexican girl from Los Angeles, and a Black girl from Oklahoma, I was never again to sense myself so solidly outside the pale of the human race. The lack of criticism evidenced by our ad hoc community influenced me, and set a tone of tolerance for my life.[10]

Then she returned to San Francisco and her mother with whom, over the years, she developed a strong relationship of mutual respect and support.

In the rush toward maturity and self-definition as a woman, Maya found herself pregnant at the age of sixteen and gave birth to her son, Guy. The next several years would see her moving from job to job, trying to keep bread on the table for her and her son.

> My son was born when I was sixteen, and determined to raise him, I had worked as a shake dancer in night clubs, fry cook in hamburger joints, dinner cook in a Creole restaurant and once had a job in a mechanic's shop taking the paint off cars with my hands.[11]

But that is far from all; she also worked as a clerk in a record shop, a chauffeur, and as the first African American conductor ever hired by the San Francisco streetcar company. Eventually, she became a successful singer and dancer, and joined a road company of the opera *Porgy and Bess*, touring throughout Europe and North Africa.

Toward the end of the 1950s, Maya moved to New York where she joined the Harlem Writers Guild, began to hone her skills as a writer, and entered the vibrant world of Black writers, artists, and social activists. At one point she became the Northern Coordinator of Dr. Martin Luther King's Southern Christian Leadership Conference. Tragically, it was on her birthday, April 4, 1968, that Dr. King was assassinated.

In 1960, Maya entered into a relationship with Vusumzi Make, a South African exile, freedom fighter and civil rights activist. She and her son Guy accompanied Make to Cairo, Egypt, where he centered his efforts to overcome apartheid. The relationship did not last, and Maya and her son moved to Ghana. She came to love Ghana and experienced it as her spiritual "homeland." She settled in the capital city of Accra, where she wrote for both the *African Review* and the *Ghanaian Times,* and taught and worked as an administrator at the School of Music of the University of Ghana where her son was a student.

In 1964, Maya returned to New York, intending to work with Malcolm X, whom she had met in Ghana. He was assassinated shortly after her return to the United States and she re-immersed herself in the black literary scene and black civil rights activism in New York.

Maya Angelou's accomplishments are many. Her online biography[12] credits her with:

Six autobiographies
Four books of personal essays
Seven children's books
Six books of poetry and several occasional poems such as *On the Pulse of Morning,* which was read at President William Clinton's inauguration
Six plays
Two screenplays

In addition to her writing, Maya Angelou has performed as an actor in more than twenty television productions and has performed in numerous films and plays. (Her performance in Alex Haley's *Roots* won her an Emmy nomination for best supporting actress.) She has made musical recordings and has written musical scores for both screenplays and the stage. As if that were not enough, Maya Angelou has also been a distinguished visiting professor at several universities and writer-in-residence at the University of Kansas.

Her online biography lists thirty-six honorary degrees and some sixty significant awards and public recognitions of her life and work, including the Mother Teresa Award for her untiring devotion and service to humanity in 2006.

Maya Angelou is indeed one "phenomenal woman."

40-DAY

Journey

WITH MAYA ANGELOU

Journey

Day 1

IS LOVE

Midwives and winding sheets
know a birthing is hard
and dying is mean
and living's a trial in between.

Why do we journey, muttering
like rumors among the stars?
Is a dimension lost?
Is it love?

~

BIBLICAL WISDOM

Why did I not die at birth,
*   come forth from the womb and expire?*
Why were there knees to receive me,
*   or breasts for me to suck?*
Now I would be lying down and quiet;
*   I would be asleep; then I would be at rest. . . .* Job 3:11-13

SILENCE FOR MEDITATION

QUESTIONS TO PONDER

- We all are born and we all will die. In what ways is life a "trial in between"? When is it not a trial?
- We have no say in where or to whom we are born. In what ways might the *accident of birth* determine the quality and promise of a person's life? Does it seem fair? Why or why not?
- Maya Angelou suggests that a lack of love lies behind the unsatisfactoriness of life that sends many on a journey through life, "muttering like rumors among the stars." Do you agree? Why or why not?

Psalm Fragment

On you I was cast from my birth,
* and since my mother bore me you have been my God.*
Do not be far from me,
* for trouble is near*
* and there is no one to help.* Psalm 22:10-11

Journal Reflections

- Write about the ways in which the accident of birth has shaped your life experiences.
- Journal about how the dimension of love is present or not present in your life.
- Make a list of the values that motivate your life and relationships, for example honesty, generosity, wealth, health. Where does love fit with your values? Is it naïve or does it make sense to suggest that love should be at the top of the list? Explain.

Prayers of Hope & Healing

Pray for those—family, friends, acquaintances, and strangers—whose life (for any reason) is a "trial in between," that they might experience the love that heals and creates a space to be and be well.

Prayer for Today

Loving God, today "where there is hatred, let me sow love."[13] Amen.

Notes

Day 2

IT IS TIME FOR THE preachers, the rabbis, the priests and pundits, and the professors to believe in the awesome wonder of diversity so that they can teach those who follow them. It is time for parents to teach young people early on that in diversity there is beauty and there is strength. We all should know that diversity makes for a rich tapestry, and we must understand that all the threads of the tapestry are equal in value no matter their color; equal in importance no matter their texture.

Our young must be taught that racial peculiarities do exist, but beneath the skin, beyond the differing features and into the true heart of being, fundamentally, we are more alike, my friend, than we are unalike.

BIBLICAL WISDOM

Parthians, Medes, Elamites, and residents of Mesopotamia, Judea and Cappadocia, Pontus and Asia, Phrygia and Pamphylia, Egypt and the parts of Libya belonging to Cyrene, and visitors from Rome, both Jews and proselytes, Cretans and Arabs—in our own languages we hear them speaking about God's deeds of power. Acts 2:9-11

SILENCE FOR MEDITATION

QUESTIONS TO PONDER

- What are the "beauty" and "strength" that can be found in diversity?
- In what ways is it true across races that we are "more alike . . . than unalike"?
- In what ways does your community of faith affirm "the awesome wonder of diversity"? Is there the potential to do more? Explain.

PSALM FRAGMENT

Praise the LORD, all you nations!
Extol him, all you peoples!
For great is his steadfast love toward us,
and the faithfulness of the LORD endures forever.
Praise the LORD! Psalm 117:1-2

JOURNAL REFLECTIONS

- Make a list of the many kinds of diversity that can be found in humankind.
- Do you believe in "the awesome wonder of diversity"? If yes, what difference does it make in the way you live? If no, why not?
- Describe a time or two when you have encountered people of other races, ethnicities, cultures, or sexual orientations. What did you learn from the encounter?

PRAYERS OF HOPE & HEALING

Pray for those who are discriminated against because of some "difference" and pray for those who discriminate, that all might recognize that "fundamentally, we are more alike . . . than unalike."

PRAYER FOR TODAY

God who created all that is, this day let me look for people who are different from me and let me celebrate and learn from the differences. Amen.

NOTES

Day 3

WHAT SETS ONE SOUTHERN TOWN apart from another, or from a Northern town or hamlet, or city high-rise? The answer must be the experience shared by the unknowing majority (it) and the knowing minority (you). All of childhood's unanswered questions must finally be passed back to the town and answered there. Heroes and bogey men, values and dislikes, are first encountered and labeled in that early environment. In later years they change faces, places and maybe races, tactics, intensities and goals, but beneath those penetrable masks they wear forever the stocking-capped faces of childhood.

BIBLICAL WISDOM

You shall put these words of mine in your heart and soul, and you shall bind them as a sign on your hand, and fix them as an emblem on your forehead. Teach them to your children, talking about them when you are at home and when you are away, when you lie down and when you rise. Write them on the doorposts of your house and on your gates, so that your days and the days of your children may be multiplied in the land. . . . Deuteronomy 11:18-21b

SILENCE FOR MEDITATION

QUESTIONS TO PONDER

- What do you think Maya Angelou means when she says that beneath the "penetrable masks" that adults present to the world you will find them forever wearing "the stocking-capped faces of childhood"? Do you think she's right? Why or why not?
- What experience was shared by the "unknowing majority" and the "knowing minority" in segregated Southern towns of the last century? To what degree does that experience continue?
- How has that shared experience created both positive and negative values, morals, and perceptions of other people in both black and white children? How have these values shaped their lives for better or for worse?

Psalm Fragment

We will not hide them from their children;
  we will tell to the coming generation
  the glorious deeds of the LORD, and his might,
  and the wonders that he has done. . . .
  that the next generation might know them,
  the children yet unborn,
  and rise up and tell them to their children. . . . Psalm 78:4, 6

Journal Reflections

- Write about the town(s) you grew up in. How did growing up in that place help to shape who you are today?
- What "unanswered questions" from your childhood remain for you? Reflect on those questions in your journal. Might the place(s) you grew up in and the people you grew up with provide clues to the answers?
- Write about how the values, morals, and perceptions of other people that you learned as a child continue to shape your life and relationships today. What, if anything, that you learned as a child have you rejected as an adult?

Prayers of Hope & Healing

Pray for those in your circle of family and friends whose childhood experiences keep them from joy, that they might experience their dignity and worth—and the dignity and worth of all others—as children of God. Give thanks for good childhood experiences that brought beauty and strength to life.

Prayer for Today

Loving God, help me to understand my roots. Let me celebrate that which was good and rise above that which was not. Amen.

Notes

Day 4

IF THE HEART OF AFRICA still remained [elusive], my search for it had brought me closer to understanding myself and other human beings. The ache for home lives in all of us, the safe place where we can go as we are and not be questioned. It impels mighty ambitions and dangerous capers. We amass great fortunes at the cost of our souls, or risk our lives in drug dens from London's Soho, to San Francisco's Haight-Ashbury. We shout in Baptist churches, wear yarmulkes and wigs and argue even the tiniest points in the Torah, or worship the sun and refuse to kill cows for the starving. Hoping that by doing these things, home will find us acceptable or failing that, that we will forget our awful yearning for it.

BIBLICAL WISDOM

They confessed that they were strangers and foreigners on the earth, for people who speak in this way make it clear that they are seeking a homeland.
Hebrews 11:13b-14

SILENCE FOR MEDITATION

QUESTIONS TO PONDER

- Maya Angelou's search for the heart of Africa was a search for "home." What do you think she means by "home"? Where is "home" for you?
- What do you think the connection might be between spirituality and the "ache for home"?
- In what ways does our culture affirm and encourage or deny and discourage the search for home?

PSALM FRAGMENT

Even the sparrow finds a home,
and the swallow a nest for herself,
where she may lay her young,
at your altars, O LORD of hosts,
my King and my God.
Happy are those who live in your house,
ever singing your praise. Psalm 84:3-4

JOURNAL REFLECTIONS

- Have you found that safe place where you can go as you are and not be questioned? If so, describe the finding and the feeling of that place. If not, can you imagine such a place?
- What kind of experiences bring you closer to understanding yourself and other human beings?
- Write about the ways in which your spirituality does (or doesn't) strengthen your sense of "home."

PRAYERS OF HOPE & HEALING

Pray for people who feel like strangers in a strange land, that they would find that safe place where they can be and belong. Give thanks for those whose "ache for home" has led them home.

PRAYER FOR TODAY

God, let me achieve such a strong sense of home that I take home with me wherever I go. Amen.

NOTES

Day 5

GUY HELD MY HAND ON the plane (on a flight from Egypt to Ghana). He leaned near and whispered, "It'll be O.K. Mom. Don't cry. I love you, Mom. Lots of people love you."

I made no attempt to explain that I was not crying because of a lack of love. . . . I was mourning all my ancestors. I had never felt that Egypt was really Africa, but now that our route had taken us across the Sahara, I could look down from my window seat and see trees, and bushes, rivers and dense forest. It all began here. The jumble of poverty-stricken children sleeping in rat-infested tenements or abandoned cars. The terrifying moan of my grandmother, "Bread of Heaven, Bread of Heaven, feed me till I want no more." The drugged days and alcoholic nights of men for whom hope had not been born. The loneliness of women who would never know appreciation or a mite's share of honor. Here, there along the banks of that river, someone was taken, tied with ropes, shackled with chains, forced to march for weeks carrying the double burden of neck irons and abysmal fear. In that large clump of trees, looking like wood moss from the plane's great height, boys and girls had been hunted like beasts, caught and tethered together. Sacrificial lambs on the altar of greed. America's period of orgiastic lynchings had begun on yonder broad savannah.

⌒

BIBLICAL WISDOM

For inquire now of bygone generations,
*   and consider what their ancestors have found;*
*   for we are but of yesterday, and we know nothing,*
*   for our days on earth are but a shadow.* Job 8:8-9

SILENCE FOR MEDITATION

QUESTIONS TO PONDER

- Reflect on Maya Angelou's poignant observation as she looked down on Africa from an airplane: "It all began here." How do you feel about her concrete examples of what began there?

- How in this new century can America continue to deal with the legacy of slavery, segregation, and the inequities of less than second-class citizenship?
- In what ways does your community of faith respond to the reality that people are still being sacrificed "on the altar of greed"? Is it enough?

PSALM FRAGMENT

I will open my mouth in a parable;
   I will utter dark sayings from of old,
   things that we have heard and known,
   that our ancestors have told us. Psalm 72:2-3

JOURNAL REFLECTIONS

- Are there any ways in which your life today is diminished or damaged by events of long ago? If not, use your journal to reflect on how distant events can bleed into present society with devastating results.
- Many people of many races and ethnicities have cause to mourn their ancestors. If that is true for you, describe the experience in your journal. If it is not true for you, talk with someone who has had that experience and record the conversation in your journal.
- Write about ways in which you or others might transform mourning into meaningful action.

PRAYERS OF HOPE & HEALING

Pray for those whose racial or ethnic history is filled with pain, that they might not be crippled by the memories, but might discover and celebrate the wisdom and goodness of their heritage.

PRAYER FOR TODAY

Holy God, like all people, I live between memories and hope; today let me honor the memories and live in the hope. Amen.

NOTES

CAGED BIRD

A free bird leaps
on the back of the wind
and floats downstream
till the current ends
and dips his wing
in the orange sun rays
and dares to claim the sky.

The free bird thinks of another
    breeze
and the trade winds soft through
    the sighing trees
and the fat worms waiting on a
    dawn-bright lawn
and he names the sky his own.

But a bird that stalks
down his narrow cage
can seldom see through
his bars of rage
his wings are clipped and
his feet are tied
so he opens his throat to sing.

But a caged bird stands on the
    grave of dreams
his shadow shouts on a nightmare
    scream
his wings are clipped and his feet
    are tied
so he opens his throat to sing.

The caged bird sings
with a fearful trill
of things unknown
but longed for still
and his tune is heard
on the distant hill

The caged bird sings
with a fearful trill
of things unknown
but longed for still
and his tune is heard
on the distant hill
for the caged bird
sings of freedom.

for the caged bird
sings of freedom.

BIBLICAL WISDOM

And God said, ". . . let birds fly above the earth across the dome of the sky."
Genesis 1:20

Silence for Meditation

Questions to Ponder

- Maya Angelou named her first autobiography *I Know Why the Caged Bird Sings*. Why do you think she would know that?
- What are the "cages" in our society and who might be called the "caged birds"?
- What are the "bars of rage" experienced by America's caged birds? What would it take to begin to open the cages?

Psalm Fragment

I know all the birds of the air,
and all that moves in the field is mine. Psalm 50:11

Journal Reflections

- Do you feel now or have you ever felt—for any reason—like a "caged bird"? If so, write in your journal why and what it feels like and what needs to be done to spring the cage open. If not, write in your journal what you think it would be like to live like a caged bird.
- Reflect on the metaphor of a "free bird" as the freedom to choose one's life, to float on the currents of one's opportunities.
- Are there any "things unknown but longed for still" in your life? If so, what keeps you from pursuing them? Can you move in their direction?

Prayers of Hope & Healing

Pray for those who live in cages, that those who don't would have the grace, courage, and moral strength to open the doors. Give thanks for those whose will and work is freedom for all.

Prayer for Today

Compassionate God, this day give me the grace to hear the caged bird singing of freedom, and the courage to do something about it. Amen.

Notes

Day 7

AFRICAN HISTORY AND CULTURE HAVE been shrouded in centuries of guilt and ignorance and shame. The African slaves themselves, separated from their tribesmen and languages, forced by the lash to speak another tongue immediately, were unable to convey the stories of their own people, their deeds, rituals, religions, beliefs. In the United States the slaves were even exiled from the drums, instruments of instruction, ceremony and entertainment of their homeland. Within a few generations details of the kingdoms of Ghana and Mali and of the Songhai Empire became hazy in their minds. The Mende concept of beauty and the Ashanti idea of justice all but faded with the old family names and intricate tribal laws. The slaves too soon began to believe what their masters believed: Africa was a continent of savages.

BIBLICAL WISDOM

The people of long ago are not remembered,
nor will there be any remembrance
of people yet to come
by those who come after them. Ecclesiastes 1:11

SILENCE FOR MEDITATION

QUESTIONS TO PONDER

- How important is it for "strangers in a strange land" to maintain a vibrant sense of their own history and culture?
- In what ways do the stories, deeds, rituals, religions, and beliefs of an ethnic community help to shape the personal identity of individuals in that community?
- What would happen to people if external forces coercively denied them access to their ethnic stories, deeds, rituals, religions, and beliefs?

Psalm Fragment

For the enemy has pursued me,
*   crushing my life to the ground,*
*   making me sit in darkness like those long dead.*
Therefore my spirit faints within me;
*   my heart within me is appalled.*
I remember the days of old,
*   I think about all your deeds,*
*   I meditate on the works of your hands.*
I stretch out my hands to you;
*   my soul thirsts for you like a parched land.* Psalm 143:3-6

Journal Reflections

- Reflect on your ethnic background. Write about the traditional stories, rituals, religions, and beliefs that are an important part of your self-identity. How is your story tied to the ancestors' stories?
- Write about the ways in which you and others in your circle of family, friends, and acquaintances maintain contact with your ethnic traditions.
- From the library or a bookstore get a book about your ethnic heritage and take notes in your journal as you read it.

Prayers of Hope & Healing

Pray for those who are unaware or ashamed of their ancestral cultural heritage, that they would find trustworthy storytellers to connect them to what is good and beautiful and true in the history of their people.

Prayer for Today

God who made and loves all peoples, today let me celebrate who I am and where I came from. Amen.

Notes

Day 8

JIMMY [AUTHOR AND PLAYWRIGHT JAMES BALDWIN, a close friend] said, "We survived slavery. Think about that. Not because we were strong. The American Indians were strong, and they were on their own land. But they have not survived genocide. You know how we survived?"

I said nothing.

"We put surviving into our poems and into our songs. We put it into our folk tales. We danced surviving in Congo Square in New Orleans and put it in our pots when we cooked pinto beans. We wore surviving on our backs when we clothed ourselves in the colors of the rainbow. We were pulled down so low we could hardly lift our eyes, so we knew, if we wanted to survive, we had better lift our own spirits. So we laughed whenever we got the chance."

BIBLICAL WISDOM

For everything there is a season, and a time for every matter under heaven: . . .
a time to weep, and a time to laugh;
a time to mourn, and a time to dance. . . . Ecclesiastes 3:1, 4

SILENCE FOR MEDITATION

QUESTIONS TO PONDER

- James Baldwin declared that the African slaves survived by putting surviving into their poems and songs, folk tales and dances, cooking and clothing. What do you think he meant?
- How important are the creative arts in encouraging and reinforcing resistance to oppression?
- In what ways does your faith community—through the Bible texts preached on, the hymns sung, and the artistic symbols of faith in the place of worship—either encourage or discourage resistance to oppression wherever it's found?

Psalm Fragment

Now my head is lifted up
  above my enemies all around me,
  and I will offer in his tent
  sacrifices with shouts of joy;
I will sing and make melody to the Lord. Psalm 27:6

Journal Reflections

- Is there a poem or song or hymn or story that has strengthened or encouraged you in a difficult time? Why did it have this effect for you?
- Write about the place of laughter in your life in times of stress and distress. Does your experience resonate with what James Baldwin said about laughter? Explain.
- In your journal try writing a poem or a song that expresses your convictions about a social justice issue that matters deeply to you.

Prayers of Hope & Healing

Pray for those whose lives are a struggle against power, that they might have poems and songs, folk tales and dances, and laughter to help them stand tall and proud.

Prayer for Today

God, regardless of the struggles I face today, may I have the wisdom to sing, dance and laugh. Amen.

Notes

Day 9

GREAT ART BELONGS TO ALL people, all the time—indeed it is made for the people by the people.

I have written of the black American experience, which I know intimately. I am always talking about the human condition in general and about society in particular. What it is like to be human, and American, what makes us weep, what makes us fall and stumble and somehow rise and go on from darkness unto darkness—that darkness carpeted with figures of fear and the hounds behind and the hunters behind and one more river to cross, and oh, my God, will I ever reach that somewhere, that safe getting-up morning. I submit to you that it is art that allows us to stand erect.

In that little town in Arkansas, whenever my grandmother saw me reading poetry she would say, "Sister, Mama loves to see you read the poetry because that will put starch in your backbone." When people who were enslaved, whose wrists were bound and whose ankles were tied, sang,

> *I'm gonna run on,*
> *See what the end is gonna be . . .*

the singer and the audience were made to understand that, however we had arrived here, under whatever bludgeoning of chance, we were the stuff out of which nations and dreams were made and that we had come here to stay.

BIBLICAL WISDOM

[B]e filled with the Spirit, as you sing psalms and hymns and spiritual songs among yourselves, singing and making melody to the Lord in your hearts. . . .
Ephesians 5:18b-19

Silence for Meditation

Questions to Ponder

- What do you think Maya Angelou means by "great art"?
- How might art help to make invisible people visible?
- Does the hymnody and liturgy in your community of faith encourage those who worship to be welcoming, hospitable, and inclusive of all people? Explain.

Psalm Fragment

Sing to him a new song;
*   play skillfully on the strings, with loud shouts.*
For the word of the LORD is upright,
*   and all his work is done in faithfulness.*
He loves righteousness and justice;
*   the earth is full of the steadfast love of the LORD.* Psalm 33:3-5

Journal Reflections

- Have there been people in your life who have encouraged you to learn a musical, literary, or graphic art? If so write about the influence their encouragement has had on you.
- Write about ways in which art puts "starch" in your backbone.
- Write about what art forms appeal to you most, speak to you most, open you most to what it means to be human.

Prayers of Hope & Healing

Pray for all those who teach and encourage the young in artistic endeavors, that they might celebrate the beauty and truth they are helping to bring into the world.

Prayer for Today

God, today let my life be a new song. Amen.

Notes

Day 10

WE MUST INFUSE OUR LIVES with art. Our national leaders must be informed that we want them to use our taxes to support street theater in order to oppose street gangs. We should have a well-supported regional theater in order to oppose regionalism and differences that keep us apart. We need nationally to support small, medium and large art museums that show us images of ourselves, those we like and those we dislike. In some way that is very important to us we need to see those we dislike even more than those we like because somehow we need at least glancing visions of how we look "as in a mirror darkly."

Our singers, composers and musicians must be encouraged to sing the song of struggle, the song of resistance, resistance to degradation, resistance to our humiliation, resistance to the eradication of all our values that would keep us going as a country. Our actors and sculptors and painters and writers and poets must be made to know that we appreciate them, that in fact it is their work that puts starch in our backbone.

We need art to live fully and to grow healthy. Without it we are dry husks drifting aimlessly on every ill wind, our futures are without promise and our present without grace.

BIBLICAL WISDOM

I call heaven and earth to witness against you today that I have set before you life and death, blessings and curses. Choose life so that you and your descendants may live. . . . Deuteronomy 30:19

SILENCE FOR MEDITATION

QUESTIONS TO PONDER

- Do you agree with Maya Angelou that "we need art to live fully and grow healthy"? Why, or why not. What for you is the difference between art and entertainment?

- Should more of our taxes be used to support art and artists? Why or why not?
- In what ways might looking at or listening to or reading artistic images of humankind that we don't like give us "at least glancing visions of how we look"?

Psalm Fragment

My mouth shall speak wisdom;
*   the meditation of my heart shall be understanding.*
I will incline my ear to a proverb;
*   I will solve my riddle to the music of the harp.* Psalm 49:3-4

Journal Reflections

- Write about a time when art taught you something important about yourself and about what it means to be human.
- In your journal write about any ways in which art has helped you to "live fully and grow healthy."
- What do you think about the relationship between art and resistance that Maya Angelou advocates? Explain.

Prayers of Hope & Healing

Pray for all artists, that their creativity would reach us and teach us how to be truly human.

Prayer for Today

Lord of the Dance, this day let whatever creativity I possess be an instrument of peace, an instrument of love. Amen.

Notes

Day 11

WHEN I THINK ABOUT MYSELF

When I think about myself,
I almost laugh myself to death,
My life has been one great big joke,
A dance that walked,
A song that spoke,
I laugh so hard I almost choke,
When I think about myself.

Sixty years in these folks' world,
The child I work for calls me girl,
I say "yes ma'am" for working's
    sake.
Too proud to bend,

Too poor to break,
I laugh until my stomach ache,
When I think about myself.

My folks can make me split my
    side,
I laughed so hard I nearly died,
The tales they tell sound just like
    lying,
They grow the fruit,
But eat the rind,
I laugh until I start to crying,
When I think about my folks.

BIBLICAL WISDOM

Even in laughter the heart is sad,
    and the end of joy is grief. Proverbs 14:13

SILENCE FOR MEDITATION

QUESTIONS TO PONDER

- What does the narrator of the poem mean when she says that her "life has been one big joke"? Does the "joke" elicit joyous laughter or bitter laughter? Why? Are there other ways of describing her laughter?
- What feelings does the image of a person's life as "A dance that walked / A song that spoke" evoke in you?
- What keeps the dance from being danced and the song from being sung?

Psalm Fragment

The days of our life are seventy years,
or perhaps eighty, if we are strong;
even then their span is only toil and trouble;
they are soon gone, and we fly away. . . .
So teach us to count our days
that we may gain a wise heart. Psalm 90:10, 12

Journal Reflections

- Explore in your journal what you think about when you think about yourself. Try writing a poem that begins with: "When I think about myself. . . ."
- Have you ever felt like your "life has been one great big joke"? If so, what caused the feeling? Anything you did—or could do—to begin living a life that makes sense to you? If you haven't felt this way, write about what you imagine it would be like.
- Write about the things/people in your life that make you laugh with joyous laughter. And about the things/people in your life that make you laugh with bitter laughter.

Prayers of Hope & Healing

Pray for those who feel that their life is a "great big joke," that they be given and take the chance to dance and sing themselves.

Prayer for Today

God, grant me the courage and grace to dance and sing myself through this day. Amen.

Notes

Day 12

The maids and doormen, factory workers and janitors who were able to leave their ghetto homes and rub against the cold-shouldered white world, told themselves that things were not as bad as they seemed. They smiled a dishonest acceptance at their mean servitude and on Saturday night bought the most expensive liquor to drown their lie. Others, locked in the unending maze of having to laugh without humor and scratch without agitation, foisted their hopes on the Lord. They shouted loudly on Sunday morning at His goodness and spent the afternoon preparing the starched uniforms to meet a boss's unrelenting examination. The timorous and the frightened held tightly to their palliatives. I was neither timid or frightened.

Biblical Wisdom

So we can say with confidence,
*   "The Lord is my helper;*
*   I will not be afraid.*
*   What can anyone do to me?"* Hebrews 13:6

Silence for Meditation

Questions to Ponder

- Karl Marx once wrote: "Religion is the sigh of the oppressed creature, the heart of a heartless world, and the soul of soulless conditions. It is the opium of the people." Do you agree, disagree, or partially agree? Explain.
- What does a community of faith need to do to be more than a "palliative" or sedative for suffering people?
- What role might religion play in the lives of oppressed people who "are neither timid or frightened"?

Psalm Fragment

Incline your ear, O Lord, and answer me,
  for I am poor and needy. . . .
Gladden the soul of your servant,
  for to you, O Lord, I lift up my soul.
For you, O Lord, are good and forgiving,
  abounding in steadfast love to all who call on you.
Give ear, O Lord, to my prayer;
  listen to my cry of supplication.
In the day of my trouble I call on you,
  for you will answer me. Psalm 86:1, 4-7

Journal Reflections

- Explore in your journal the ways in which your spirituality equips you to face the harsher realities of life.
- Write about the practices you follow to nurture your spirituality.
- Write about the role of your faith community in providing comfort, strength, and hope for living through dark times.

Prayers of Hope & Healing

Pray for communities of faith—especially your own—that they would comfort, strengthen, encourage, and equip people to challenge injustice and not simply sedate them to the pain of injustice.

Prayer for Today

Gracious God, let me find the comfort, strength, and hope I need in your house among people of faith, and give me the courage to live that hope outside your house. Amen.

Notes

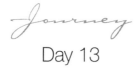

Day 13

ANOTHER DAY WAS OVER. IN the soft dark the cotton truck spilled the pickers out and roared out of the yard with a sound like a giant's fart. The workers stepped around in circles for a few seconds as if they had found themselves in an unfamiliar place. Their minds sagged.

In the Store the men's faces were the most painful to watch, but I seemed to have no choice. When they tried to smile to carry off their tiredness as if it were nothing, the body did nothing to help the mind's attempt at disguise. Their shoulders drooped even as they laughed, and when they put their hands on their hips in a show of jauntiness, the palms slipped the thighs as if the pants were waxed.

"Evening Sister Henderson. Well, back where we started, huh?"

"Yes sir, Brother Stewart. Back where you started, bless the Lord."

Momma [Maya Angelou's grandmother] could not take the smallest achievement for granted. People whose history and future were threatened each day by extinction considered that it was only by divine intervention that they were able to live at all. I find it interesting that the meanest life, the poorest existence, is attributed to God's will, but as human beings become more affluent, as their living standard and style begin to ascend the material scale, God descends the scale of responsibility at a commensurate speed.

BIBLICAL WISDOM

Why did I come forth from the womb
to see toil and sorrow,
and spend my days in shame? Jeremiah 20:18

SILENCE FOR MEDITATION

QUESTIONS TO PONDER

- How would you describe the differences between work that enhances one's sense of personal dignity and work that debases one's sense of personal dignity?

- Do you agree with Maya Angelou that the poor whose lives are precarious at best are more likely to credit divine intervention for their survival while the affluent whose lives are comfortable are more likely to credit themselves for their good fortune? Why, or why not?
- Why do you think that Maya Angelou's grandmother "couldn't take the smallest achievement for granted"?

PSALM FRAGMENT

Have mercy upon us, O LORD, have mercy upon us,
*   for we have had more than enough of contempt.*
Our soul has had more than its fill
*   of the scorn of those who are at ease,*
*   of the contempt of the proud.* Psalm 123:3-4

JOURNAL REFLECTIONS

- Reflect in your journal on your work. In what ways does it (or does it not) enhance your sense of self-worth and personal dignity?
- What role do you think God plays in the up times and down times of your life?
- Maya Angelou's grandmother was a strong woman whose values and character helped shape Maya's values and character. If there have been such people in your life, write about them in your journal.

PRAYERS OF HOPE & HEALING

Pray for those who do the menial tasks in our world that must be done, that they and their work would be met with respect and fair compensation.

PRAYER FOR TODAY

God, today let me have the humility and grace to show respect to people I meet whose hard and often manual labor keeps the wheels of society turning. Amen.

NOTES

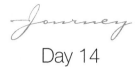

Day 14

BEFORE TELEVISION BROUGHT PICTURES OF luxurious living rooms and glistening kitchens into the view of the impoverished, they could pretend, tell themselves that only the few, the lucky, maybe just their employers, lived lives of refined comfort.

But today, when every soap opera is rife with characters whose great wealth is only equaled by their moral neediness, paupers watching in shacks on every street are forced to admit that they are indeed poverty-stricken.

With that knowledge and acknowledgment, there comes inevitably a lingering despair and a puzzling wretchedness. Why them and not me? Those questions are followed by a sense of worthlessness—a remorseful regret at being alive. Then comes full-blown anger, resentment, a rankling bitterness that, if directed outward can foment riots, revolution and social chaos. Most often, however, the convulsions of anger are directed inward. Thus the poor, the needy, the misfits of society implode. After the debris settles, they appear to the onlookers as dry husks of hopelessness.

If it is true that a chain is only as strong as its weakest link, isn't it also true a society is only as healthy as its sickest citizen and only as wealthy as its most deprived?

I believe so.

<hr />

BIBLICAL WISDOM

I hate, I despise your festivals,
*   and I take no delight in your solemn assemblies. . .*
Take away from me the noise of your songs;
*   I will not listen to the melody of your harps.*
But let justice roll down like waters,
*   and righteousness like an ever-flowing stream.* Amos 5:21, 23-24

SILENCE FOR MEDITATION

Questions to Ponder

- If you were speaking to a poor person, how would you respond to the question "Why them and not me?"
- What is the responsibility of faith communities over against grinding poverty?
- What is the difference between justice and charity?

Psalm Fragment

Let me hear what God the LORD will speak,
for he will speak peace to his people,
to his faithful, to those who turn to him in their hearts.
Steadfast love and faithfulness will meet;
righteousness and peace will kiss each other. Psalm 85:8, 10

Journal Reflections

- Write about what feelings are evoked in you when you watch the lives of the rich and famous on television or in movies.
- Reflect in your journal on Maya Angelou's observation that "a society is only as healthy as its sickest citizen and only as wealthy as its most deprived."
- If you have ever had an occasion, either professionally or as a volunteer, to work with the poor or disadvantaged, reflect on the experience.

Prayers of Hope & Healing

Pray for our political, religious, economic, and social institutions, that they would begin talking about and then taking the concrete moral and structural steps necessary to end poverty.

Prayer for Today

God of compassion, "let me not so much seek to be consoled as to console, to be understood as to understand, to be loved as to love."[14] Amen.

Notes

Day 15

FIRST I HAD TO UNDERSTAND the thinking of the Savages [a street gang]. They were young black men, preying on other young black men. They had been informed, successfully, that they were worthless, and everyone who looked like them was equally without worth. Each sunrise brought a day without hope and each evening the sun set on a day lacking achievement. Whites, who ruled the world, owned the air and food and jobs and schools and fair play, had refused to share with them any of life's necessities—and somewhere, deeper than their consciousness, they believed the whites were correct. They, the black youth, young lords of nothing, were born without value and would creep, like blinded moles, their lives long in the darkness, under the earth, chewing on roots, driven far from light.

BIBLICAL WISDOM

Are not five sparrows sold for two pennies? Yet not one of them is forgotten in God's sight. But even the hairs of your head are all counted. Do not be afraid; you are of more value than many sparrows. Luke 12:6-7

SILENCE FOR MEDITATION

QUESTIONS TO PONDER

- In what ways can street gangs of any race become surrogate families?
- Maya Angelou is suggesting that all too often the oppressed cooperate with their oppression. Do you agree? Why, or why not?
- Is anyone truly "born without value"? If some come to believe that about themselves what can be done?

Psalm Fragment

When I look at your heavens, the work of your fingers,
the moon and the stars that you have established;
what are human beings that you are mindful of them,
mortals that you care for them?
Yet you have made them a little lower than God,
and crowned them with glory and honor. Psalm 8:3-5

Journal Reflections

- Write about your sense of self-worth and value. What makes you feel good about yourself?
- Reflect on your youth. Did you develop a good sense of self-worth and personal value? If so, who and what helped you develop that sense? If not, what worked against your development of self-worth and value?
- In what, if any ways, does your spirituality contribute to your feelings of self-worth and value?

Prayers of Hope & Healing

Pray for the young, especially those who are troubled or disadvantaged, that they may be found by adults who believe in them.

Prayer for Today

God of great compassion, let me find a kid to befriend and mentor. Amen.

Notes

Day 16

SOMEHOW AND FOR SOME VAGUE and inane reason, we have decided it is better to be exploited, misused, battered and bedraggled than to become disagreeable. We think that possibly the brute, who is prepared to treat a victim in the most unkind way, will be coerced into being more kind if the victim is courteous. I don't agree. If I am attacked, when I have done nothing to warrant an attack, or even if I have, I work myself up into a fury much more explosive than the miscreant can imagine. I jump into a righteous lather. And I mean to make myself more to deal with than the brute can handle. I mean if I can make myself get mad before I get scared the evildoer will rue the day.

BIBLICAL WISDOM

So then, putting away falsehood, let all of us speak the truth to our neighbors, for we are members of one another. Be angry but do not sin; do not let the sun go down on your anger. . . . Ephesians 4:25-26

SILENCE FOR MEDITATION

QUESTIONS TO PONDER

- It might seem like Maya Angelou's advice runs counter to Jesus' teaching that we should love our enemies and pray for those who persecute us. Does it? Explain.
- How would you distinguish between righteous anger and unrighteous anger?
- How do you understand "be angry but do not sin"? Is this good advice for people who are concerned with justice issues? Why, or why not?

Psalm Fragment

Rise up, O Lᴏʀᴅ, in your anger;
 lift yourself up against the fury of my enemies;
 awake, O my God; you have appointed a judgment. Psalm 7:6

Journal Reflections

- Do you handle anger well or does anger handle you? Explain.
- Have you ever responded when unjustly attacked—or been tempted to respond—the way Maya Angelou suggests? If so, explore the experience in your journal. If not, write about how you do respond to unjust attacks.
- Make a list of the things/situations/people who make you angry. Explore the reasons for your anger in your journal. How do you typically respond to those things/situations/people?

Prayers of Hope & Healing

Pray and give thanks for those whose anger is kindled by injustice, that they would find creative ways to use that anger in the cause of justice.

Prayer for Today

Holy and righteous God, if I get angry today let it be for the right reasons, and let me not let the sun go down on my anger. Amen.

Notes

Day 17

BEING A WOMAN IS HARD work. Not without joy or even ecstasy, but still relentless, unending work. . . .

The woman who survives intact and happy must be at once tender and tough. She must have convinced herself, that she, her values, and her choices are important. In a time and world where males hold sway and control, the pressure upon women to yield their rights-of-way is tremendous. And it is under those very circumstances that the woman's toughness must be in evidence.

She must resist considering herself a lesser version of her male counterpart. She is not a sculptress, poetess, authoress, Jewess, Negress, or even (now rare) in university parlance a rectoress. If she is the thing, then for her own sense of self and for the education of the ill-informed she must insist with rectitude in being the thing and in being called the thing.

A rose by any other name may smell as sweet, but a woman called by a devaluing name will only be weakened by the misnomer.

ح

BIBLICAL WISDOM

So God created humankind in his image,
in the image of God he created them;
male and female he created them. Genesis 1:27

SILENCE FOR MEDITATION

QUESTIONS TO PONDER

- How does the "pressure upon women to yield their rights-of-way" manifest itself in our society? Are men ever pressured to yield their rights-of-way?
- In what ways does our culture endorse and promote sexist attitudes, conditions, and behaviors?
- Given these realities, what does it mean to say that "under those very circumstances . . . the woman's toughness must be in evidence"?

Psalm Fragment

On the day I called, you answered me,
* you increased my strength of soul.* Psalm 138:3

Journal Reflections

- If you are a woman, write about whether or not you are surviving "intact and happy."
- If you are a man, explore your attitudes and behaviors towards women in your journal. Write about whether or not you are surviving "intact and happy" as a man.
- Using today's *Biblical Wisdom* text as a springboard, write about how you think male/female relationships should work.

Prayers of Hope & Healing

Pray for all women and men, that we may all truly see the worth, dignity, and essential equality that belong to all of us as people created in the image of God.

Prayer for Today

Gracious God, let my faith in your creative love create in me a reverence for all life. Amen.

Notes

Day 18

THE BLACK MOTHER PERCEIVES DESTRUCTION at every door, ruination at each window, and even she herself is not beyond her own suspicion. She questions whether she loves her children enough—or more terribly, does she love them too much? Do her looks cause embarrassment—or even more terrifying, is she so attractive her sons begin to desire her and her daughters begin to hate her. If she is unmarried, the challenges are increased. Her singleness indicates that she has rejected, or has been rejected by her mate. Yet she is raising children who will become mates. Beyond her door, all authority is in the hands of people who do not look or think or act like her and her children. Teachers, doctors, sales clerks, librarians, policemen, welfare workers are white and exert control over her family's moods, conditions and personality; yet within the home, she must display a right to rule which at any moment, by a knock at the door, or a ring of the telephone can be exposed as false. In the face of these contradictions, she must provide a blanket of stability, which warms but does not suffocate, and she must tell her children the truth about the power of white power without suggesting that it cannot be challenged.

BIBLICAL WISDOM

"Honor your father and mother"—this is the first commandment with a promise: "so that it may be well with you and you may live long on the earth." Ephesians 6:2

SILENCE FOR MEDITATION

QUESTIONS TO PONDER

- Do you think that Maya Angelou's depiction of the black mother might also apply to other minority mothers in our white dominant culture? Explain.

- Today's reading comes from Maya Angelou's autobiography *The Heart of a Woman,* which narrates her experience during her thirties in the 1960s. In what ways do you think the experience of black mothers might have changed since then? How might it still be the same?
- What do you think Maya Angelou means when she says the black mother "must tell her children the truth about the power of white power without suggesting that it cannot be challenged"?

Psalm Fragment

Once God has spoken;
twice have I heard this:
that power belongs to God,
and steadfast love belongs to you, O Lord. Psalm 62:11-12a

Journal Reflections

- In your journal, look back on your childhood and youth, and write about the challenges your mother faced in raising you.
- If you are a mother or father, write about the ways in which Maya Angelou's description of the black mother do (or do not) resonate with your own experience.
- Make a list of the significant, mentoring adults who helped guide and shape you. Write a brief letter to each in your journal expressing your gratitude. If it is possible and seems good to you, copy your letter onto stationary and mail it to them.

Prayers of Hope & Healing

Pray for mothers and fathers, grandmothers and grandfathers, and mentors, that they may see the fruit of their love in the children they raise and guide into life.

Prayer for Today

God of mercy, help me to feel and find ways to express gratitude to those who have guided me along the way. Amen.

Notes

Day 19

SOME PEOPLE WHO EXIST SPARINGLY on the mean side of the hill are threatened by those who also live in the shadows but celebrate the light.

It seems easier to lie prone than to press against the law of gravity and raise the body onto its feet and persist in remaining vertical.

There are many incidents which can eviscerate the stalwart and bring the mighty down. In order to survive, the ample soul needs refreshments and reminders daily of its right to be and to be wherever it finds itself.

I was fired from a job when I was sixteen years old and was devastated. My entire personal worth was laid waste. My mother found me crying in my upstairs room. (I had left the door ajar, hoping for consolation.)

She tapped at the door and stepped in. When she asked why I was crying, I told her what happened.

Her face suddenly became radiant with indulgent smiles. She sat down on my bed and took me into her arms.

"Fired? Fired?" She laughed. "What the hell is that? Nothing. Tomorrow you'll go looking for another job. That's all."

She dabbed at my tears with her handkerchief. "So what? Remember, you were looking for a job when you found the one you just lost. So you'll just be looking for a job one more time."

She laughed at her wisdom and my consternation. "And think about it, if you ever get fired again, the boss won't be getting a cherry. You've been through it once and survived."

⁓

BIBLICAL WISDOM

Your eye is the lamp of your body. If your eye is healthy, your whole body is full of light; but if it is not healthy, your body is full of darkness. Therefore consider whether the light in you is not darkness. If then your whole body is full of light, with no part of it in darkness, it will be as full of light as when a lamp gives you light with its rays. Luke 11:34-36

Silence for Meditation

Questions to Ponder

- Why is it that "some people who exist sparingly on the mean side of the hill are threatened by those who also live in the shadows but celebrate the light"?
- What is an "ample soul"? In what ways—and why—does an "ample soul" show itself in humor.
- Is a person born with an "ample soul" or can such a soul be cultivated and nurtured? Explain.

Psalm Fragment

But I have calmed and quieted my soul,
*   like a weaned child with its mother;*
*   my soul is like the weaned child that is with me.* Psalm 131:2

Journal Reflections

- Do you consider yourself to have an "ample soul"? Why, or why not? Write about the ways in which your soul shows itself.
- Do you know anyone who lives in the shadows but celebrates the light? Write about that person. What have you learned from him or her?
- Write about a time when you sought consolation and perhaps a new perspective on a problem from someone. Write about a time when you consoled someone who was down in the dumps.

Prayers of Hope & Healing

Give thanks for mothers and fathers and friends who bring consolation, perspective, and humor into the lives of children and friends.

Prayer for Today

Loving God, no matter how deep the shadows, give me the grace to celebrate the light. Amen.

Notes

Day 20

HE [MARTIN LUTHER KING JR.] began to speak in a rich sonorous voice. . . . A lot of you, he reminded us [in New York], are from the South and still have ties to the land. Somewhere there was an old grandmother holding on, a few uncles, some cousins and friends. He said the South we might remember is gone. There was a new South. A more violent and ugly South, a country where our white brothers and sisters were terrified of change, inevitable change. They would rather scratch up the land with bloody fingers and take their most precious document, The Declaration of Independence, and throw it in the deepest ocean, bury it under the highest mountain, or burn it in the most flagrant blaze, than admit justice into a seat at the welcome table, and fair-play room in a vacant inn. . . .

The Reverend King continued, chanting, singing his prophetic litany. We were one people, indivisible in the sight of God, responsible to each other and for each other.

We, the black people, the most displaced, the poorest, the most maligned and scourged, we had the glorious task of reclaiming the soul and saving the honor of the country. We, the most hated, must take hate into our hands and by the miracle of love, turn loathing into love. We, the most feared and apprehensive, must take fear and by love, change it into hope. We, who die daily in large and small ways, must take the demon death and turn it into life.

His head was thrown back and his words rolled out with the rumbling of thunder. We had to pray without ceasing and work without tiring. We had to know evil will not forever stay on the throne. That right, dashed to the ground, will rise, rise again and again.

BIBLICAL WISDOM

Those who say, "I love God," and hate their brothers or sisters, are liars; for those who do not love a brother or sister whom they have seen, cannot love God whom they have not seen. The commandment we have from him is this: those who love God must love their brothers and sisters also. 1 John 4:20-21

SILENCE FOR MEDITATION

QUESTIONS TO PONDER

- Martin Luther King, Jr. was a proponent of non-violent resistance to evil. Do you agree with his strategy? Why, or why not?
- King argued for the brotherhood and sisterhood of all people regardless of race or class. What are the practical implications of this position?
- Is it naïve to suppose that love, hope, and prayer can be effective tactics against oppression and injustice? Explain.

PSALM FRAGMENT

Which of you desires life,
and covets many days to enjoy good?
Keep your tongue from evil,
and your lips from speaking deceit.
Depart from evil, and do good;
seek peace, and pursue it. Psalm 34:12-14

JOURNAL REFLECTIONS

- Record your reaction to Dr. King's words as recorded by Maya Angelou. How do they make you feel?
- If you have ever participated in a march or protest against injustice or have engaged in non-violent civil disobedience in the struggle for justice, write about the experience.
- If you have not had such experiences, what might move you to participate in the future? What might hinder you from participating in the future?

PRAYERS OF HOPE & HEALING

Give thanks for those who risk themselves in the struggle for justice, and pray that their passion might bear fruit.

PRAYER FOR TODAY

Father/Mother God, open my eyes to see that the folks around me are my folks, sisters and brothers. Amen.

NOTES

Day 21

THE AFRICAN WOMEN SAT ENRAPTURED as I spoke of Sojourner Truth. I related the story of the six-foot tall ex-slave speaking at an equal rights meeting of white women in the 1800s. That evening a group of white men in the hall, already incensed that their own women were protesting sexism, were livid when a black woman rose to speak. One of the town's male leaders shouted from the audience: "I see the stature of the person speaking and remark the ferocious gestures. I hear the lowness and timbre of the speaker's voice. Gentlemen, I am not convinced that we are being addressed by a woman. Indeed, before I will condone further speech by that person, I must insist that some of the white ladies take the speaker into the inner chamber and examine her and then I will forbear to listen."

The other men yelled their agreement, but the white women refused to be a party to such humiliation.

Sojourner Truth, however, from the stage took the situation in hand. In a booming voice which reached the farthest row in the large hall, she said:

"Yoked like an ox, I have plowed your land. And ain't I a woman? With axes and hatchets, I have cut your forests and ain't I a woman? I gave birth to thirteen children and you sold them away from me to be the property of strangers and to labor in strange lands. Ain't I a woman? I have suckled your babes at this breast." Here she put her large hands on her bodice. Grabbing the cloth she pulled. The threads gave way, the blouse and her undergarments parted and her huge tits hung pendulously free. She continued, her face unchanging and her voice never faltering, "And ain't I a woman?"

BIBLICAL WISDOM

There is no longer Jew or Greek, there is no longer slave or free, there is no longer male and female; for all of you are one in Christ Jesus. Galatians 3:28

Silence for Meditation

Questions to Ponder

- What feelings were evoked in you while reading Sojourner Truth's rejoinder to the men who tried to humiliate her?
- Clearly racism is not the only evil "ism" in our society. Besides sexism, what other "isms" do you think need to be tackled?
- How might the faith and resources of a community of faith be used in challenging the "isms" that plague our society?

Psalm Fragment

Search me, O God, and know my heart;
test me and know my thoughts.
See if there is any wicked way in me,
and lead me in the way everlasting. Psalm 139:23-24

Journal Reflections

- If you have been hurt by any of society's "isms," explore the experience in your journal.
- If you look at others through the lens of any of society's "isms," wonder about that in your journal. Do you know why you do? How do you feel about it? Any desire to change? If so, how would you go about it?
- If you are a woman, write about what it means to you to be a woman. If you are a man, write about what it means to you to be a man.

Prayers of Hope & Healing

Give thanks for any and all who challenge the isms that diminish, damage, and sometimes destroy others' lives, that they may not lose heart.

Prayer for Today

Gracious God, grant me the grace to see people as people and not as labels. Amen.

Notes

Day 22

My God. My world was spinning off its axis, and there was nothing to hold on to. Anger and haughtiness, pride and prejudice, my old back-up team would not serve me in this new predicament. These whites were treating me as an equal, as if I could do whatever they could do. They did not consider that race, height, or gender or lack of education might have crippled me and that I should be regarded as someone invalided.

The old habits of withdrawing into righteous indignation or lashing out furiously against insults were not applicable in this circumstance.

Oh, the holiness of always being the injured party. The historically oppressed can find not only sanctity but safety in the state of victimization. When access to a better life has been denied often enough, and successfully enough, one can use the rejection as an excuse to cease all efforts. After all, one reckons, "they" don't want me, "they" accept their own mediocrity and refuse my best, "they" don't deserve me. And, finally, *I* am better, kinder, truer than "they," even if I behave badly and act shamefully. And if I do nothing, I have every right to my idleness, for, after all, haven't I tried?

Biblical Wisdom

We are afflicted in every way, but not crushed; perplexed, but not driven to despair; persecuted, but not forsaken; struck down, but not destroyed. . . .
2 Corinthians 4:8-9

Silence for Meditation

Questions to Ponder

- In what ways do you think it would be difficult for the "historically oppressed" to shed the role of victim?
- Do you think there is a difference between being "victimized" and being a "victim"? Can you experience the former and not become the latter? Explain.

- There is a tragicomic element in today's Maya Angelou reading. What do you make of it?

Psalm Fragment

Our steps are made firm by the Lord,
  when he delights in our way;
  though we stumble, we shall not fall headlong,
  for the Lord holds us by the hand. Psalm 37:23-24

Journal Reflections

- Write about those situations, if any, where you are you tempted to reduce people to "they" and "me" or "they" and "we."
- If you have ever discovered that someone you thought looked down on you really didn't (or saw you quite differently from the way you imagined they did), explore the experience in your journal.
- Have you or anyone you know ever taken refuge in the "state of victimization"? If so, explore the experience in your journal. If not, write about what you imagine such an experience would feel like.

Prayers of Hope & Healing

Pray for those in your circle of family, friends, acquaintances, and colleagues who are stuck in stereotypes of themselves or of others, that they may have an "aha" experience that takes them to new levels of understanding and relationship.

Prayer for Today

Holy God, let me treat myself and others today with the dignity due to the children of God. Amen.

Notes

Day 23

SAVIOR

Petulant priests, greedy
centurions, and one million
incensed gestures stand
between your love and me.

Your *agape* sacrifice
is reduced to colored glass,
vapid penance, and the
tedium of ritual.

Your footprints yet
mark the crest of
billowing seas but

your joy
fades upon the tablets
of ordained prophets.

Visit us again, Savior.

Your children burdened with
disbelief, blinded by a patina
of wisdom,
carom down this vale of
fear. We cry for you
although we have lost
your name.

BIBLICAL WISDOM

Woe to you, scribes and Pharisees, hypocrites! For you tithe mint, dill, and cumin, and have neglected the weightier matters of the law: justice and mercy and faith. It is these you ought to have practiced without neglecting the others. You blind guides! You strain out a gnat but swallow a camel! Woe to you, scribes and Pharisees, hypocrites! For you clean the outside of the cup and of the plate, but inside they are full of greed and self-indulgence. You blind Pharisee! First clean the inside of the cup, so that the outside also may become clean. Matthew 23:23-26

SILENCE FOR MEDITATION

QUESTIONS TO PONDER

- In what if any ways might the church with all its hierarchies and trappings be an obstacle to spirituality and a deep encounter with Christ?

- What is Maya Angelou asking for when she prays: "Visit us again, Savior"?
- What does it mean to pray "We cry for you / although we have lost / your name"?

PSALM FRAGMENT

O God, you are my God, I seek you,
my soul thirsts for you;
my flesh faints for you,
as in a dry and weary land where there is no water. Psalm 63:1

JOURNAL REFLECTIONS

- Have you ever been burned or bored or burdened by the church? If so, write about the experience and where it has left you spiritually. If not, write about the role of the church in your spirituality.
- Write about where, how, and with whom you have your deepest encounters with God.
- Is there anything or anyone who stands between Christ's love and you? Explain.

PRAYERS OF HOPE & HEALING

Pray for the leaders of your community of faith (and all religious leaders) that they might be so filled with God that God bleeds through them into the world.

PRAYER FOR TODAY

Holy God, let nothing and no one "stand / between your love and me." Amen.

NOTES

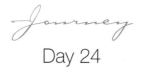

Day 24

ON AN EVENING WALK ALONG Fillmore, Clyde [Maya Angelou's son] and I heard a loud shouting and saw a group of people crowded around a man on the corner across the street. We stopped where we were to listen.

"Lord, we your children. We come to you just like newborn babies. Silver and gold have we none. But O Lord!"

Clyde grabbed my hand and started to pull me in the opposite direction.

"Come on, Mom. Come on."

I bent down to him. "Why?"

"That man is crazy." Distaste wrinkled his little face.

"Why do you say that?"

"Because he's shouting in the street like that."

I stooped to my son giving no attention to the passers-by. "That's one of the ways people praise God. Some praise in church, some in the streets, and some in their hearts."

"But Mom, is there really a God? And what does he do all the time?"

The question deserved a better answer than I could think of in the middle of the street. I said, "We'll talk about it later, but now let's go over and listen. Think of the sermon as a poem and the singing as great music."

He came along and I worked my way through the crowd so he could have a clear view. The antics of the preacher and the crowd's responses embarrassed him. I was stunned. I had grown up in a Christian Methodist Episcopal Church where my uncle was superintendent of Sunday School and my grandmother was Mother of the Church. Until I was thirteen and left Arkansas for California, each Sunday I spent a minimum of six hours in church. . . . And my son asked me if there was a God. To whom had I been praying all my life?

That night I taught him "Joshua Fit the Battle of Jericho."

Biblical Wisdom

The fear of the Lord is the beginning of wisdom,
and the knowledge of the Holy One is insight. Proverbs 9:10

Silence for Meditation

Questions to Ponder

- How would you react to a street preacher like the one in Maya Angelou's story? Why?
- If a child asked you "Is there really a God? And what does he do all the time?" how would you answer?
- Why do you think that after this experience Maya Angelou taught her son "Joshua Fit the Battle of Jericho?"

Psalm Fragment

The fear of the Lord is the beginning of wisdom;
all those who practice it have a good understanding. Psalm 111:10

Journal Reflections

- Write about the ways and places in which you praise God.
- Make a list of the forms of religious expression you are comfortable with. Also make a list of the kinds of religious expression you find uncomfortable. How might you explore outside your comfort zone?
- Write a letter to whoever has most influenced your spiritual formation. Express your gratitude for their guidance and tell them how it is with you now spiritually. If it seems good to you and is possible, send them the letter.

Prayers of Hope & Healing

Give thanks for people in your life who have been humbly unafraid to talk with you about their faith and spiritual practices.

Prayer for Today

God, let my life be a song of praise to you in the way I live and love. Amen.

Notes

Day 25

SPIRIT IS AN INVISIBLE FORCE made visible in all life. In many African religions there is the belief that all things are inhabited by spirits which must be appeased and to which one can appeal. So, for example, when a master drummer prepares to carve a new drum, he approaches the selected tree and speaks to the spirit residing there. In his prayer he describes himself, his experience, and his expertise; then he explains his intent. He insures the spirit that he will remain grateful for the gift of the tree and that he will use the drum only for honorable purposes.

I believe that Spirit is one and is everywhere present. That it never leaves me. That in my ignorance I may withdraw from it, but I can realize its presence the instant I return to my senses.

It is this belief in a power larger than myself and other than myself which allows me to venture into the unknown and even the unknowable. I cannot separate what I conceive as Spirit from my concept of God. Thus, I believe that God is Spirit.

~

BIBLICAL WISDOM

Jesus said to her, "Woman, believe me, the hour is coming when you will worship the Father neither on this mountain nor in Jerusalem. You worship what you do not know; we worship what we know, for salvation is from the Jews. But the hour is coming, and is now here, when the true worshipers will worship the Father in spirit and truth, for the Father seeks such as these to worship him. God is spirit, and those who worship him must worship in spirit and truth." John 4:21-24

SILENCE FOR MEDITATION

QUESTIONS TO PONDER

- Maya Angelou says that "Spirit is an invisible force made visible in all life." How do you think Spirit becomes visible?
- How do you (or don't you) resonate with Maya Angelou's description of the master drummer?

- Do you agree with Maya Angelou that "Spirit is one and everywhere present"? If so, how does that belief shape the way you are in the world? If not, what is your belief about Spirit?

PSALM FRAGMENT

Where can I go from your spirit?
Or where can I flee from your presence?
If I ascend to heaven, you are there;
*   if I make my bed in Sheol, you are there.*
If I take the wings of the morning
*   and settle at the farthest limits of the sea,*
*   even there your hand shall lead me,*
*   and your right hand shall hold me fast.* Psalm 139:7-10

JOURNAL REFLECTIONS

- Write about a time, place, situation when you were conscious of the Spirit's presence.
- Maya Angelou states that "belief in a power larger than myself and other than myself . . . allows me to venture into the unknown and even the unknowable." Write about a time when your faith allowed you to "venture into the unknown."
- Explore in your journal what it takes to return you to your senses and an awareness of Spirit at times when you have lost that awareness.

PRAYERS OF HOPE & HEALING

Give thanks for those who are able to see Spirit in all life and who thus reverence and care for all life.

PRAYER FOR TODAY

Spirit God, open me and keep me open to your everywhere presence. Amen.

NOTES

Day 26

WHILE I KNOW MYSELF AS a creation of God, I am also obligated to realize and remember that everyone else and everything else are also God's creation. This is particularly difficult for me when my mind falls upon the cruel person, the batterer, and the bigot. I would like to think that the mean-spirited were created by another force and under the aegis and direction of something other than my God. But since I believe that God created all things, I am not only constrained to know that the oppressor is a child of God, but also obliged to treat him or her as a child of God.

My faith is tested many times every day, and more times than I'd like to confess, I'm unable to keep the banner of faith aloft. If a promise is not kept, or a secret is betrayed, or if I experience long-lasting pain, I begin to doubt God and God's love. I fall so miserably into the chasm of disbelief that I cry out in despair. Then the Spirit lifts me up again, and once more I am secured in faith. I don't know how that happens, save when I cry out earnestly I am answered immediately and am returned to faithfulness. I am once again filled with Spirit and firmly planted on solid ground.

BIBLICAL WISDOM

But I say to you that listen, Love your enemies, do good to those who hate you, bless those who curse you, pray for those who abuse you. Luke 6:27-28

SILENCE FOR MEDITATION

QUESTIONS TO PONDER

- Does it trouble you to consider that those who do evil are as much children of God as anyone else? Why, or why not?
- What are the ethical implications of believing that you along with everyone and everything else are God's creation?

- In a world like ours, is Jesus' advice in today's *Biblical Wisdom* naïve and foolish or profound and practical? Explain.

PSALM FRAGMENT

Hear, O LORD, when I cry aloud,
  be gracious to me and answer me!
"Come," my heart says, "seek his face!"
  Your face, LORD, do I seek. Psalm 27:7-8

JOURNAL REFLECTIONS

- Write about the ways in which your faith is (or has been) tested. What do you do in the face of such testing?
- Where or to whom do you turn when you find yourself falling "into the chasm of disbelief"?
- Make a list of the people you have the most difficulty praying for. Write about your reasons. Try praying for them even if it is simply to commit them into the care of God.

PRAYERS OF HOPE & HEALING

Pray for those in your circle of family, friends, colleagues, and acquaintances who seem to be struggling between faith and disbelief, that they might rest in the grace of a God who is not afraid of our questions.

PRAYER FOR TODAY

Spirit of God, if I fall today, lift me up and secure me in faith. Amen.

NOTES

Day 27

MANY THINGS CONTINUE TO AMAZE me, even well into the sixth decade of my life. I'm startled or taken aback when people walk up to me and tell me they are Christians. My first response is the question "Already?" It seems to me a lifelong endeavor to try to live the life of a Christian. I believe that is also true for the Buddhist, for the Muslim, for the Jainist, for the Jew, and for the Taoist who try to live their beliefs. The idyllic condition cannot be arrived at and held on to eternally. It is in the search itself that one finds the ecstasy.

BIBLICAL WISDOM

Not everyone who says to me, 'Lord, Lord,' will enter the kingdom of heaven, but only the one who does the will of my Father in heaven. Matthew 7:21

SILENCE FOR MEDITATION

QUESTIONS TO PONDER

- From your perspective, what exactly is a Christian?
- Why is the charge of hypocrisy so often leveled at religious people?
- Maya Angelou implies that faith should be a way of life, not just a way of belief. Do you agree? Why, or why not?

PSALM FRAGMENT

Good and upright is the LORD;
    therefore he instructs sinners in the way.
He leads the humble in what is right,
    and teaches the humble his way.
All the paths of the LORD *are steadfast love and faithfulness,*
    for those who keep his covenant and his decrees. Psalm 25:8-10

Journal Reflections

- Write about the relationship between your faith and the daily decisions you make.
- As a person of faith, how would you describe yourself? As a believer? As a seeker? As on the journey? As following a way or a path? In some other way? Explain.
- Maya Angelou believes "it is in the search itself that one finds the ecstasy." What do you think she means by "ecstasy"? Have you found the "ecstasy"? If so, journal about the experience. If not, where do you think it might be found?

Prayers of Hope & Healing

Pray that all people of faith would have the grace and humility to confess that they are on the way and have not yet fully arrived.

Prayer for Today

God, I am on the way to you; walk with me. Amen.

Notes

Day 28

WHEN I THINK OF DEATH, and of late the idea has come with alarming frequency, I seem at peace with the idea that a day will dawn when I will no longer be among those living in this valley of strange humors. I can accept the idea of my own demise, but I am unable to accept the death of anyone else. I find it impossible to let a friend or relative go into that country of no return. Disbelief becomes my close companion, and anger follows in its wake.

I answer the heroic question "death, where is thy sting?" with "It is here in my heart and mind and memories."

I am besieged with painful awe at the vacuum left by the dead. Where did she go? Where is she now? Are they, as the poet James Weldon Johnson said, "resting in the bosom of Jesus"? If so, what about my Jewish loves, my Japanese dears, my Muslim darlings? Into whose bosom are they cuddled? There is always, lurking quietly, the question of what certainty is there that I, even I, will be gathered into the gentle arms of the Lord. I start to suspect that only with such blessed assurance will I be able to allow death its duties.

⌐

BIBLICAL WISDOM

When this perishable body puts on imperishability, and this mortal body puts on immortality, then the saying that is written will be fulfilled:
   "Death has been swallowed up in victory."
   "Where, O death, is your victory?
   Where, O death, is your sting?" 1 Corinthians 15:54-55

SILENCE FOR MEDITATION

Questions to Ponder

- What attitudes toward death does our culture promote? Do you feel they are healthy or unhealthy attitudes?
- Angelou states that she "can accept the idea of my own demise, but I am unable to accept the death of anyone else." Do you resonate with her experience? Why, or why not?
- Maya Angelou raises the important question of Christian exclusivity. What about her "Jewish loves," her "Japanese dears," her "Muslim darlings"? Into whose bosom are they cuddled?

Psalm Fragment

Precious in the sight of the LORD
  is the death of his faithful ones. Psalm 116:15

Journal Reflections

- Explore in your journal what you think of when you think of death. Are you able to "allow death its duties"? Why, or why not?
- Maya Angelou writes: "I answer the heroic question 'death, where is thy sting?' with 'It is here in my heart and mind and memories.'" Would you answer the question the same way? Explain.
- Has the death of a close loved one left a "vacuum" in your life? If so, write a letter to him or her in your journal expressing your feelings and what they meant to you.

Prayers of Hope & Healing

Pray that the "heart and mind and memories" of those who lose a loved one would encounter the comforting presence of God's Spirit.

Prayer for Today

God, let me live fully and joyfully knowing that "it is in dying that we are born to eternal life."[15] Amen.

Notes

IN THE BIBLICAL STORY, THE prodigal son risked and for a time lost everything he had because of an uncontrollable hunger for company. First, he asked for and received his inheritance, not caring that his father, from whom he would normally inherit, was still alive; not considering that by demanding his portion, he might be endangering the family's financial position. The parable relates that after he took the fortune, he went off into a far country and there he found company. Wasteful living conquered his loneliness and riotous companions conquered his restlessness. For a while he was fulfilled, but he lost favor in the eyes of his friends. As the money began to disappear he began to slip down that deep road to social oblivion.

His condition became so reduced that he began to have to feed the hogs. Then it further worsened until he began to eat with the hogs. It is never lonesome in Babylon. Of course, one needs to examine who—or in the prodigal son's case, what—he has for company.

Many people remind me of the journey of the prodigal son. Many believe that they need company at any cost, and certainly if a thing is desired at any cost, it will be obtained at all costs.

We need to remember and to teach our children that solitude can be a much-to-be-desired condition. Not only is it acceptable to be alone, at times it is positively to be wished for.

It is in the interludes between being in company that we talk to ourselves. Then we ask questions of ourselves. We describe ourselves to ourselves, and in the quietude we may even hear the voice of God.

᧒

BIBLICAL WISDOM

Then Jesus said, "There was a man who had two sons. The younger of them said to his father, 'Father, give me the share of the property that will belong to me.' So he divided his property between them. A few days later the younger son gathered all he had and traveled to a distant country, and there he squandered his property in dissolute living." Luke 15:11-13

Silence for Meditation

Questions to Ponder

- Maya Angelou uses the story of the prodigal son to argue for the need for solitude to overcome the distractions of constant, often unhelpful company. Do you agree with her use of the story? Why, or why not?
- Do you think our society encourages or discourages solitude? Explain.
- Does your community of faith encourage or discourage solitude as a spiritual practice? Explain.

Psalm Fragment

For God alone my soul waits in silence,
for my hope is from him. Psalm 62:5

Journal Reflections

- Explore in your journal whether you are comfortable or uncomfortable with silence and solitude.
- Do silence and solitude play a role in your spiritual practice? If so, how? If not, why not?
- In your journaling, what questions do you ask of yourself? How do you describe yourself to yourself? What have you heard of the voice of God?

Prayers of Hope & Healing

Pray that those who are always in company would discover the delights of solitude and that those who favor solitude would discover the delights of company.

Prayer for Today

God, in times of quiet let me learn more of myself and more of you. Amen.

Notes

Day 30

IN MY TWENTIES IN SAN Francisco I became a sophisticate and an acting agnostic. It wasn't that I had stopped believing in God; it's just that God didn't seem to be around the neighborhoods I frequented. And then a voice teacher introduced me to *Lessons in Truth*, published by the Unity School of Christianity.

One day the teacher, Frederick Wilkerson, asked me to read to him. I was twenty-four, very erudite, very worldly. He asked that I read from *Lessons in Truth*, a section which ends with these words "God loves me." I read the piece and closed the book, and the teacher said, "Read it again." I pointedly opened the book , and I sarcastically read, "God loves me." He said, "Again." After about the seventh repetition I began to sense that there might be some truth in the statement, that there was a possibility that God really did love me. Me, Maya Angelou. I suddenly began to cry at the grandness of it all. I knew that if God loved me, then I could do wonderful things, I could try great things, learn anything, achieve anything. For what could stand against me with God, since one person, any person with God, constitutes the majority.

BIBLICAL WISDOM

Beloved, since God loved us so much, we also ought to love one another. No one has ever seen God; if we love one another, God lives in us, and his love is perfected in us. 1 John 4: 11-12

SILENCE FOR MEDITATION

QUESTIONS TO PONDER

- What do you make of Maya Angelou's statement that "God didn't seem to be around the neighborhoods I frequented"?
- What kinds of questions do poverty, oppression, injustice, and consequent human suffering raise about the love and goodness and presence of God? How would you answer those questions?

- What does it mean to say that "one person, any person with God, constitutes the majority"?

PSALM FRAGMENT

By day the LORD commands his steadfast love,
  and at night his song is with me,
  a prayer to the God of my life. Psalm 42:8

JOURNAL REFLECTIONS

- Has it ever seemed to you that God is not around in the places where you live and work and play? If so, explore the feeling in your journal.
- Close this book, and for the next ten or fifteen minutes keep repeating, "God loves me." Open your journal and reflect on the experience.
- Do you practice meditation or centering prayer? If so, try using the word "love" as your "sacred word" for the next few months, and record your experience in your journal. If not, why not give it a try?[16]

PRAYERS OF HOPE & HEALING

Give thanks for teachers and mentors and writers and artists who gently lead their students toward truth.

PRAYER FOR TODAY

God of great love, help me to know that, even when I feel unloved, I am yet loved, and it makes a world of difference. Amen.

NOTES

Day 31

FOR HUNDREDS OF YEARS, THE Black American slaves had seen the parallels between their oppression and that of the Jews in Biblical times.

Go down Moses
Way down in Egypt land
Tell old Pharaoh
To let my people go.

The prophets of Israel inhabited our songs:

Didn't my Lord deliver Daniel?
Then why not every man?

Ezekiel saw the wheel, up in the middle of the air.

Little David play on your harp.

The Hebrew children in the fiery furnace elicited constant sympathy from the black community because our American experience mirrored their ancient tribulation.

BIBLICAL WISDOM

Then the LORD said, "I have observed the misery of my people who are in Egypt; I have heard their cry on account of their taskmasters. Indeed, I know their sufferings, and I have come down to deliver them from the Egyptians, and to bring them up out of that land to a good and broad land, a land flowing with milk and honey. . . . The cry of the Israelites has now come to me; I have also seen how the Egyptians oppress them. So come, I will send you to Pharaoh to bring my people, the Israelites, out of Egypt. Exodus 3:7-8a, 9-10

Silence for Meditation

Questions to Ponder

- Think about the situations, times, places, and occasions in which the Bible has been used to give hope and courage to the oppressed.
- Think about the situations, times, places, and occasions in which the Bible has been used to sanction and strengthen oppressors.
- Are there dominant themes in the Bible that would give precedence to either of these two ways of reading the Bible? Explain.

Psalm Fragment

I am the LORD your God,
who brought you up out of the land of Egypt. Psalms 81:10

Journal Reflections

- Make a list of your favorite passages/stories from the Bible. How do these passages help shape your self-understanding?
- How do these passages and stories from the Bible help shape your personal morality and public ethics?
- Try writing a "psalm" which expresses the main themes of your favorite biblical texts.

Prayers of Hope & Healing

Pray for all those who interpret and proclaim the message of the Bible for our time, that they would seek and teach that truth with humility and with openness to the often unconventional guidance of God's Spirit.

Prayer for Today

"Let the words of my mouth and the meditation of my heart be acceptable to you, O LORD, my rock and my redeemer" (Psalm 19:14). Amen.

Notes

Day 32

PREACHER, DON'T SEND ME

Preacher, don't send me
when I die
to some big ghetto
in the sky
where the rats eat cats
of the leopard type
and Sunday brunch
is grits and tripe.

I've known those rats
I've seen them kill
and grits I've had
would make a hill,
or maybe a mountain,
so what I need
from you on Sunday
is a different creed.

Preacher, please don't
promise me
streets of gold
and milk for free.
I stopped all milk
at four years old
and once I'm dead
I won't need gold.

I'd call a place
pure paradise
where families are loyal
and strangers are nice,
where the music is jazz
and the season is fall.
Promise me that
or nothing at all.

BIBLICAL WISDOM

"See, the home of God is among mortals.
He will dwell with them;
   they will be his peoples,
   and God himself will be with them;
   he will wipe every tear from their eyes.
   Death will be no more;
   mourning and crying and pain will be no more,
   for the first things have passed away."
And the one who was seated on the throne said, "See, I am making all things
new." Revelation 21: 3-5

Silence for Meditation

Questions to Ponder

- Oppressed people often hear a "pie-in-the-sky-bye-and-bye" theology from both their oppressors and their own preachers. What is the "different creed" the poem calls for?
- The poet rejects both a "more of the same" heaven (which the rich might well hope for) and a "pie-in-the-sky" heaven. Reflect on stanza four. What is she calling for?
- In stanza four the poet seems to suggest that "heaven" should begin in the here and now. If so, what is she asking of the "preacher"?

Psalm Fragment

Let this be recorded for a generation to come,
so that a people yet unborn may praise the LORD:
that he looked down from his holy height,
from heaven the LORD looked at the earth,
to hear the groans of the prisoners,
to set free those who were doomed to die. . . . Psalm 102:18-20

Journal Reflections

- Write about how you envision the afterlife.
- Write about whether or not the teachings of your community of faith about death and the afterlife relate to your daily life.
- Reflect on the often-heard criticism of religion that it is "so heavenly minded that it is no earthly good." Fair? Unfair? Somewhere in between?

Prayers of Hope & Healing

Pray for all those crying out for a full and abundant life right here, right now, that they might get it.

Prayer for Today

God of justice, today let me work, live, and play in paradise with you. Amen.

Notes

Day 33

THERE ARE SOME WHO ARE so frightened by the idea of sensual entertainment that they make even their dwelling places bleak and joyless. And what is horrible is that they would have others share that lonely landscape. Personally, I'll have no part of it. I want all my senses engaged.

I would have my ears filled with the world's music, the grunts of hewers of wood, the cackle of old folks sitting in the last sunlight and the whir of busy bees in the early morning. I want to hear the sharp sound of tap dancing and the mournful murmur of a spiritual half remembered and then half sung. I want the clashing cymbals of a marching band and the whisper of a lover entreating a beloved. Let me hear anxious parents warning their obstreperous offspring and a pedantic pedagogue teaching a bored class the mysteries of thermodynamics. All sounds of life and living, death and dying are welcome to my ears.

My eyes will gladly receive colors; the burnt-orange skin of old black women who ride on buses and the cool lavender of certain people's eyes. I like the tomato-red dresses of summer and the sienna of a highly waxed mahogany table. I love the dark green of rain forests and the sunshine yellow of a bowl of lemons. Let my eager sight rest on the thick black of a starless night and the crisp white of fresh linen. And I will have blue. The very pale blue of some complexions and the bold blue of flags. The iridescent blue of hummingbird wings and the dusty blue twilight in North Carolina. I am not daunted by the blood-red of birth and the red blood of death. My eyes absorb the world's variety and uniqueness.

~

BIBLICAL WISDOM

The flowers appear on the earth;
the time of singing has come,
and the voice of the turtledove
is heard in our land.
The fig tree puts forth its figs,
and the vines are in blossom;
they give forth fragrance. Song of Songs 2:12-13a

Silence for Meditation

Questions to Ponder

- Why do you suppose that some people are "frightened by the idea of sensual entertainment"?
- Do you agree with Maya Angelou that "all sounds of life and living, death and dying" are the "world's music"? Explain.
- Why would it be a good thing to be fully attentive/mindful of all the world's music and color? What do they teach?

Psalm Fragment

It is good to give thanks to the LORD,
to sing praises to your name, O Most High;
to declare your steadfast love in the morning,
and your faithfulness by night,
to the music of the lute and the harp,
to the melody of the lyre. Psalm 92:1-3

Journal Reflections

- Are you frightened or excited by sensual experience? Explain.
- Explore in your journal whether you are so distracted by responsibilities, duties and schedules that your senses are numb to the sensual. Or are you mindful enough of your surroundings that your senses are fully engaged?
- Write about what of the "world's music" really turns you on. What of the world's colors turn you on?

Prayers of Hope & Healing

Give thanks for all the world's music and all the world's color, and for the ability to be moved by it all.

Prayer for Today

Lord of the Dance, open me to the world's music and let it be for me the soundtrack to life, accompaniment to my joys and sorrows. Amen.

Notes

Day 34

Taste and smell are firmly joined in wedded bliss. About the bliss I cannot speak, but I can say much about that marriage. I like it that the fleeting scent of fresh-cut citrus and the flowery aroma of strawberries will make my salivary glands pour into my mouth a warm and pure liquid. I accept the salt of tears evoked by sweet onions and betrayed love. Give me the smell of the sea and the wild scent of mountain pines. I do not spurn the suffocating smell of burned rubber of city streets nor the scent of fresh sweat because their pungency reminds me of the bitterness of chocolate and the sting of vinegar. Some of life's greatest pleasures are conveyed by the dual senses of taste and smell.

In this tribute to sensuality I have saved the sense of touch as the last pleasure to be extolled. I wish for the slick feel of silk underclothes and the pinch of sand in my beach shoes. I welcome the sun strong on my back and the tender pelting of snow on my face. Good clothes that fit snugly without squeezing and strong fearless hands that caress without pain. I want the crunch of hazelnuts between my teeth and ice cream melting on my tongue.

Biblical Wisdom

Awake, O north wind,
and come, O south wind!
Blow upon my garden
that its fragrance may be wafted abroad.
Let my beloved come to his garden,
and eat its choicest fruits. Song of Songs 4:16

Silence for Meditation

Questions to Ponder

- In what ways does our society appeal to human sensuality for good? For ill?
- How does your religious tradition treat the sensual? How are taste, touch, smell, hearing, and sight a part of the worship experience?
- Sensuality has been thought immoral by some and amoral by others. Do you think that sensuality has a moral dimension? Explain.

Psalm Fragment

You cause the grass to grow for the cattle,
    and plants for people to use,
    to bring forth food from the earth,
    and wine to gladden the human heart,
    oil to make the face shine,
    and bread to strengthen the human heart. Psalm 104:14-15

Journal Reflections

- Write about which of your five senses seem most highly attuned and easily engaged. How does that play out in the way you do life?
- Write about which of your five senses seems least attuned and often unengaged. How does that play out in the way you do life?
- Write about how, if at all, your sensuality integrates with your spirituality.

Prayers of Hope & Healing

Pray for all those so busy and distracted that they live mostly in their heads, that they might come to their senses.

Prayer for Today

Creator God, let me be mindful today of all I see and hear and taste and smell and touch, and in all that, let me see, hear, taste, smell and touch your mystery. Amen.

Notes

Day 35

... I REALIZE that living well is an art that can be developed. Of course, you will need the basic talents to build upon: They are a love of life and ability to take great pleasure from small offerings, an assurance that the world owes you nothing and that every gift is exactly that, a gift. That people who may differ from you in political stance, sexual persuasion, and racial inheritance can be founts of fun, and if you are lucky, they can become even convivial comrades.

Living life as art requires a readiness to forgive. I do not mean that you should suffer fools gladly, but rather remember your own shortcomings, and when you encounter another with flaws, don't be eager to righteously seal yourself away from the offender forever. Take a few breaths and imagine yourself having committed the action which has set you at odds.

Because of the routines we follow, we often forget that life is an ongoing adventure. We leave our homes for work, acting and even believing that we will reach our destination with no unusual event startling us out of our set expectations. The truth is we know nothing, not where our cars will fail or when our buses will stall, whether our places of employment will be there when we arrive, or whether, in fact, we ourselves will arrive whole and alive at the end of our journeys. Life is pure adventure, and the sooner we realize that, the quicker we will be able to treat life as art: to bring all our energies to each encounter, to remain flexible enough to notice and admit when what we expected to happen did not happen. We need to remember that we are created creative and can invent new scenarios as frequently as they are needed.

BIBLICAL WISDOM

So when you are offering your gift at the altar, if you remember that your brother or sister has something against you, leave your gift there before the altar and go; first be reconciled to your brother or sister, and then come and offer your gift.
Matthew 5:23-24

Silence for Meditation

Questions to Ponder

- In what sense can it be said that "living well is an art," that living well engages our creativity?
- Do you agree that people you have sharp differences with can become "founts of fun" and "even convivial comrades"?
- Maya Angelou states that "we are created creative and can invent new scenarios as frequently as they are needed." Do you find that exciting? Frightening? A bit of both?

Psalm Fragment

You show me the path of life.
In your presence there is fullness of joy;
*   in your right hand are pleasures forevermore.* Psalm 16:11

Journal Reflections

- Would you consider yourself a "life artist"? Why, or why not?
- Make a list of people with whom your relationships are troubled because of different political stances, religious views, social ideologies, sexual persuasion, or racial/ethnic inheritance. Try to envision ways to positively recreate those relationships. Can it be done? If so, how? If not, why not?
- Explore in your journal whether you essentially see life as "an ongoing adventure" or prefer life as a set of dependable routines.

Prayers of Hope & Healing

Give thanks for the creativity that enables us to envision and shape new relationships and a new world.

Prayer for Today

God, where there is despair let me bring hope, where there is darkness, light.[17] Amen.

Notes

Day 36

EACH OF US HAS THE right and the responsibility to assess the roads which lie ahead, and those over which we have traveled, and if the future road looms ominous or unpromising, and the roads back uninviting, then we need to gather our resolve and, carrying only the necessary baggage, step off that road into another direction. If the new choice is also unpalatable, without embarrassment, we must be ready to change that as well.

~

BIBLICAL WISDOM

Thus says the LORD:
  Stand at the crossroads, and look,
  and ask for the ancient paths,
  where the good way lies; and walk in it,
  and find rest for your souls. Jeremiah 6:16

SILENCE FOR MEDITATION

QUESTIONS TO PONDER

- Why is it so difficult to change course, to take a new path, to go in a new direction?
- What is the "necessary baggage" that we need to carry when we step off the road we have been traveling and head off in a new direction?
- Why is it important to make new life choices "without embarrassment"? What attitudes and beliefs would help someone to do that?

PSALM FRAGMENT

Your word is a lamp to my feet
  and a light to my path. Psalm 119:10

Journal Reflections

- In your journal assess the road(s) that brought you to where you are today. Are you satisfied with them? Dissatisfied? Somewhere in between?
- Assess the road(s) that presently lie before you. Are you satisfied with them? Dissatisfied? Somewhere in between?
- Does your assessment of the roads behind you and the roads presently before you suggest that you stay the course or chart a new direction? If a new direction seems called for, sketch it out in your journal and began planning how to change course.

Prayers of Hope & Healing

Pray for those whose lives are cast in the concrete of routines, that their creativity would bubble up and break the mold.

Prayer for Today

Guiding God, when there is more than one road ahead, give me the wisdom to choose the one headed in the right direction for me so I don't simply choose the way of least resistance. Amen.

Notes

Day 37

THERE IS AN IMMUTABLE LIFE principle with which many people will quarrel.

Although nature has proven season in and season out that if the thing that is planted bears at all, it will yield more of itself, there are those who seem certain that if they plant tomato seeds, at harvest time they can reap onions.

Too many times for comfort I have expected to reap good when I known I have sown evil. My lame excuse is that I have not always known that actions can only reproduce themselves, or rather, I have not always allowed myself to be aware of that knowledge. Now, after years of observation and enough courage to admit what I have observed, I try to plant peace if I do not want discord; to plant loyalty and honesty if I want to avoid betrayal and lies.

Of course, there is no absolute assurance that those things I plant will always fall upon arable land and will take root and grow, nor can I know if another cultivator did not leave contrary seeds before I arrived. I do know, however, that if I leave little to chance, if I am careful about the kinds of seeds I plant, about their potency and nature, I can, within reason, trust my expectations.

⁓

BIBLICAL WISDOM

Do not be deceived; God is not mocked, for you reap whatever you sow.
Galatians 6:7

SILENCE FOR MEDITATION

QUESTIONS TO PONDER

- How is the "immutable life principle" that Maya Angelou writes about affirmed and/or denied by your experience or the experience of someone you know?

- Do you agree that "if [you are] careful about the kinds of seeds [you] plant, about their potency and nature, [you] can, within reason, trust [your] expectations"? Why, or why not?
- Why is it that most if not all religious traditions seem to be storehouses for both good and evil seeds?

PSALM FRAGMENT

Those who go out weeping,
  bearing the seed for sowing,
  shall come home with shouts of joy,
  carrying their sheaves. Psalm 126:6

JOURNAL REFLECTIONS

- Record in your journal the ways in which your life does or does not reflect the life principle Maya Angelou writes about: you reap what you sow.
- Make a list of the kind of seeds you *want* to sow. Circle any that you normally do not take the time, effort or expense to sow.
- Reflect back on the last twenty-four hours. What kind of seeds have you planted? What has been the harvest?

PRAYERS OF HOPE & HEALING

Pray for those who sow love and peace and encouragement and hope and beauty and truth, that their seeds would sprout and grow strong and bear much fruit.

PRAYER FOR TODAY

Holy God, let me sow good seed and share the harvest. Amen.

NOTES

Day 38

CURIOUS, BUT WE HAVE COME to a place, a time, when virtue is no longer considered a virtue. The mention of virtue is ridiculed, and even the world itself has fallen out of favor. Contemporary writers rarely employ such words as *purity, temperance, goodness, worth,* or even *moderation.* Students, save those enrolled in philosophy courses or studying in seminaries, seldom encounter questions on morality and piety.

We need to examine what the absence of those qualities has done to our communal spirit, and we must learn how to retrieve them from the dust heap of nonuse and return them to a vigorous role in our lives.

Nature will not abide a vacuum, and because we have let the positive particulars go, they have been replaced with degeneracy, indifference, and vice. Our streets explode with cruelty and criminality, and our homes are rife with violence and abuse. Too many of our leaders shun the higher moral road and take the path to satisfy greed while they voice hollow rhetoric.

BIBLICAL WISDOM

The fruit of the Spirit is love, joy, peace, patience, kindness, generosity, faithfulness, gentleness, and self-control. There is no law against such things. Galatians 5:22-23

SILENCE FOR MEDITATION

QUESTIONS TO PONDER

- Is it true that "we have come to a place, a time, when virtue is no longer considered a virtue"? Why, or why not?
- If you agree that virtue is largely absent in our culture, what has its absence "done to our communal spirit?"
- If you believe that virtue is largely present in our culture, what are convincing signs of its presence?

Psalm Fragment

Happy are those
  who do not follow the advice of the wicked,
  or take the path that sinners tread,
  or sit in the seat of scoffers;
  but their delight is in the law of the LORD,
  and on his law they meditate day and night. Psalm 1:1-2

Journal Reflections

- How important are personal morality and piety or spirituality to you? Reflect in your journal on how that level of importance is reflected in your day-to-day life.
- Make a list of what you consider to be essential personal and public virtues. Which of them are you strongly committed to? Explain.
- Alongside your list of virtues, make a list of each virtue's opposite. Do any of them characterize your way of being in the world? Explain.

Prayers of Hope & Healing

Pray that those who teach and preach morality might do so without sliding down the slippery slope of moralism and legalism.

Prayer for Today

Righteous God, let me live in such a way that is good for me and good for others. Amen.

Notes

Day 39

THE NEW TESTAMENT INFORMS THE reader that it is more blessed to give than to receive. I have found that among its other benefits, giving liberates the soul of the giver. The size and substance of the gift should be important to the recipient, but not to the donor save that the best thing one can give is that which is appreciated. The giver is as enriched as is the recipient, and more important, that intangible but very real psychic force of good in the world is increased.

When we cast our bread upon the waters, we can presume that someone downstream whose face we will never know will benefit from our action, as we who are downstream from another will profit from that grantor's gift.

Since time is the one immaterial object which we cannot influence—neither speed up nor slow down, add to nor diminish—it is an imponderably valuable gift. Each of us has a few minutes a day or a few hours a week which we could donate to an old folks' home or a children's hospital ward. The elderly whose pillows we plump or whose water pitchers we refill may or may not thank us for our gift, but the gift is upholding the foundation of the universe. The children to whom we read simple stories may or may not show gratitude, but each boon we give strengthens the pillars of the world.

BIBLICAL WISDOM

The point is this: the one who sows sparingly will also reap sparingly, and the one who sows bountifully will also reap bountifully. Each of you must give as you have made up your mind, not reluctantly or under compulsion, for God loves a cheerful giver. 2 Corinthians 9:6-7

SILENCE FOR MEDITATION

Questions to Ponder

- Do you agree that "giving liberates the soul of the giver"? Why, or why not?
- In what ways might giving increase "that intangible but very real psychic force of good in the world"?
- Do you agree that plumping pillows for the elderly or reading a story to a child upholds "the foundation of the universe" and "strengthens the pillars of the world"? Why, or why not?

Psalm Fragment

Happy are those who consider the poor. . . . Psalm 41:1a

Journal Reflections

- If you have experienced the liberation of your soul through the act of giving, write about the experience in your journal. What was your soul liberated from?
- What giving have you done in the last month or so that has upheld the foundation of the universe?
- Is your volunteerism occasional or regular? Do you think it's enough? Why, or why not?

Prayers of Hope & Healing

Give thanks for those who volunteer their time and abilities and resources to improve the lives of others.

Prayer for Today

God, may the way I use my time and talents and money reflect your boundless compassion for a hurting world. Amen.

Notes

Day 40

EVERY PERSON NEEDS TO TAKE one day away. A day in which one consciously separates the past from the future. Jobs, lovers, family, employers, and friends can exist one day without any one of us, and if our egos permit us to confess, they could exist eternally in our absence.

Each person deserves a day away in which no problems are confronted, no solutions searched for. Each of us needs to withdraw from the cares which will not withdraw from us. We need hours of aimless wandering or spates of time sitting on park benches, observing the mysterious world of ants and the canopy of treetops.

If we step away for a time, we are not, as many may think and some will accuse, being irresponsible, but rather we are preparing ourselves to more ably perform our duties and discharge our obligations.

BIBLICAL WISDOM

Now during those days he went out to the mountain to pray; and he spent the night in prayer to God. Luke 6:12

SILENCE FOR MEDITATION

QUESTIONS TO PONDER

- Do you think it's true that "jobs, lovers, family, employers, and friends can exist one day without any one of us"? If so, is that a liberating or frightening thought? If not, why not?
- Why is it that in our society so many Americans do not take all (or any) of their vacation? Are you like that? Why, or why not?
- Do you agree that a day away spent in "aimless wandering," or "sitting on park benches," or just doing what you enjoy doing is not irresponsible? Explain.

PSALM FRAGMENT

Be still, and know that I am God! Psalm 46:10a

JOURNAL REFLECTIONS

- What, if any, are the cares which will not withdraw from you? Explore them in your journal and wonder if a day away might give you a new perspective on them.
- Which duties and obligations would you be more able to perform if you had a day away?
- If you had "a day away in which no problems are confronted, no solutions searched for," what would you do? Go for it! And then record your day away in your journal.

PRAYERS OF HOPE & HEALING

Give thanks for occasional times for yourself and others in which to simply be and not do.

PRAYER FOR TODAY

God help me to realize that I am not so important that I have to be constantly connected, constantly busy, constantly productive, constantly doing something. Amen.

NOTES

Journey's End

You have finished your *40-Day Journey with Maya Angelou.* I hope it has been a good journey and that along the way you have learned much, experienced much and found good resources to deepen your understanding, faith and practice. As a result of this journey:

- How are you different?
- What have you learned?
- What have you experienced?
- In what ways has your understanding, faith and practice been transformed?

NOTES

For Further Reading

ESSAYS

Wouldn't Take Nothing For My Journey Now. New York: Bantam Books, 1994.

Even the Stars Look Lonesome. New York: Bantam Books, 1998.

POETRY

The Complete Collected Poems of Maya Angelou. New York: Random House, 1994.

AUTOBIOGRAPHIES

The Collected Autobiographies of Maya Angelou. New York: Modern Library, 2004.

Sources

CA indicates the page number in *The Collected Autobiographies of Maya Angelou*

CP indicates the page number in *The Complete Collected Poems of Maya Angelou*

Day 1:   *Is Love*, CP 228
Day 2:   *Wouldn't Take Nothing For My Journey Now*, 126
Day 3:   *I Know Why the Caged Bird Sings*, CA 20
Day 4:   *All God's Children Need Traveling Shoes*, CA 1041
Day 5:   *The Heart of a Woman*, CA 864
Day 6:   *Caged Bird*, CP 194
Day 7:   *Even the Stars Look Lonesome*, 15
Day 8:   *A Song Flung Up to Heaven*, CA 1160
Day 9:   *Even the Stars Look Lonesome*, 130-31
Day 10: *Even the Stars Look Lonesome*, 133
Day 11: *Just Before the World Ends*, CP 29
Day 12: *Gather Together in My Name*, CA 371
Day 13: *I Know Why the Caged Bird Sings*, CA 94
Day 14: *Even the Stars Look Lonesome*, 107-08
Day 15: *The Heart of a Woman*, 697
Day 16: *Even the Stars Look Lonesome*, 117
Day 17: *Wouldn't Take Nothing For My Journey Now*, 6-7
Day 18: *The Heart of a Woman*, CA 655
Day 19: *Wouldn't Take Nothing For My Journey Now*, 80
Day 20: *The Heart of a Woman*, CA 673-74
Day 21: *The Heart of a Woman*, CA 751
Day 22: *Singin' and Swingin' and Gettin' Merry Like Christmas*, CA 461

NOTES

1   Maya Angelou, *Wouldn't Take Nothing For My Journey Now* in *The Complete Autobiographies of Maya Angelou* (New York: Modern Library, 2004), 80.

2   Sharon Burt, "Maya Angelou," http://voices.cla.umn.edu/vg/Bios/entries/angelou_maya.html, 1998

3   Maya Angelou, "Is Love," *I Shall Not Be Moved* in *The Complete Collected Poems of Maya Angelou* (New York: Random House, 1994), 228.

4   James Baldwin, book cover copy for *The Complete Collected Poems of Maya Angelou*.

5   Maya Angelou, "Phenomenal Woman," *And Still I Rise* in *The Complete Collected Poems of Maya Angelou*, 130.

6   Maya Angelou, *I Know Why the Caged Bird Sings,* in *The Collected Autobiographies of Maya Angelou*, 49.

7   Ibid., 74.

8   Ibid.

9   Ibid., 78.

10 Ibid., 195.

11 Singin' and *Swingin' and Gettin' Merry Like Christmas*, in *The Collected Autobiographies of Maya Angelou*, 414.

12 http://www.mayaangelou.com/longbiography.html

13 From a prayer attributed to St. Francis of Assisi.

14 Ibid.

15 Ibid.

16 For an introduction to centering prayer, see: Basil Pennington, *Centering Prayer: Renewing an Ancient Christian Prayer Form* (New York: Doubleday, 2001) and Basil Pennington and Thomas Keating, *Finding Grace at the Center: The Beginning of Centering Prayer* (Woodstock, Vermont: Skylight Paths, 2002)

17 Paraphrase of a prayer attributed to St. Francis of Assisi.

NOTES